P9-DFZ-283

Asperger Syndrome
and Difficult Moments

Asperger Syndrome and Difficult Moments

Practical Solutions for Tantrums, Rage, and Meltdowns

Brenda Smith Myles
and
Jack Southwick

AAPC

Autism Asperger Publishing Co.
P.O. Box 23173
Shawnee Mission, Kansas 66283-0173

© 1999 by Autism Asperger Publishing Co.
P.O. Box 23173
Shawnee Mission, Kansas 66283-0173

All rights reserved. No part of the material protected by this copyright notice may be reproduced or used in any form or by any means, electronic or mechanical, including photocopying, recording, or by any information storage and retrieval system, without the prior written permission of the copyright owner.

Publisher's Cataloging-in-Publication
(provided by Quality Books, Inc.)

Myles, Brenda
    Asperger syndrome and difficult moments : practical
solutions for tantrums, rage, and meltdowns / Brenda
Smith Myles, Jack Southwick – 1st ed.
    p. cm.
    Includes bibliographic references and index.
    Library of Congress Catalog Card Number: 99-73141
    ISBN: 0-9672514-3-5

    1. Asperger's syndrome. 2. Anger.
I. Southwick, Jack. II. Title.

RC553.A88M97 1999   616.89'82
                    QBI99-1234

This book was previously published under the title
*Asperger Syndrome and Rage : Practical Solutions for
a Difficult Moment*

This book is designed in Minion, Helvetica Neuland
Extended, and Ellington

Managing Editor: Kirsten McBride
Cover Design: Taku Hagiwara
Production Assistant: Ginny Biddulph
Interior Design/Production: Tappan Design

Printed in the United States of America

Dedicated to the children
at Camp Determination,
who were the
inspiration for this book.

Contents

CHAPTER 1

An Overview of the Characteristics of Asperger Syndrome That May Impact Behavior

In 1944, Hans Asperger, an Austrian physician, described the unique characteristics of four children he had seen in his clinic. These children had a common disturbance, which Asperger defined in the context of (a) physical appearance and expressive characteristics, (b) intelligence, (c) behavior within a social group, and (d) drive and affect. Disturbances in these areas hindered the children in effectively engaging in social interactions at an early age. Asperger noted that even though these children experienced social deficits, they were capable of original thoughts and experiences that could lead to exceptional achievements and eventual social acceptability.

Over time, Asperger made some changes in his original conceptualization of the children he studied. However, the essential clinical characteristics remained the same. Asperger's work was primarily dormant until Wing (1981) brought attention to this exceptionality. In her seminal paper, she discussed Asperger's work and further elaborated by providing 34 case studies that showed surprising similarities to Asperger's findings. Since then, a number of studies and anecdotes have described and defined characteristics that have come to be referred to as Asperger Syndrome. Many of the essential descriptors outlined by Asperger remained the same, leading researchers and writers such as Frith (1991) and Wing (1981) to conclude that Asperger's characterizations have withstood the test of time.

Over the past few years, this neurological disorder has increasingly been recognized by professionals and parents, particularly since the addition of Asperger Syndrome in the *International Classification of Diseases and Related Health Problems* (World Health Organization, 1992) (see Table 1.1) and *Diagnostic and Statistical Manual – 4th Edition* (American Psychological Association, 1994) (see Table 1.2). According to these documents, to receive a diagnosis of Asperger Syndrome, an individual must exhibit some atypical form of repetitive patterns of behavior, interests and activities. These behaviors can include but are not limited to: (a) an encompassing preoccupation in one or more areas of interest, (b) an inflexible adherence to a nonfunctional routine or ritual, (c) repetitive motor movements, or (d) a persistent preoccupation with parts of objects.

The following provides a brief discussion of specific characteristics related to Asperger Syndrome in the areas of (a) cognition, (b) language, (c) socialization, (d) sensory issues, (e) visual processing, and (f) behavior.

Cognition

Over 50 years ago, Asperger reported an adult-like intellectual functioning in the children he observed related to a limited number of special interests. That is, these children looked at things from a different viewpoint and thought about problems that were far beyond the perceived interests or the intellectual level of same-age peers.

Currently, researchers and practitioners recognize that although the vast majority of students with Asperger Syndrome have average to above-average intellectual abilities and are included in general education classrooms, they experience academic problems. Indeed, social and communication deficits combined with obsessive and narrowly defined interests, concrete and literal thinking, inflexibility, poor problem-solving and organizational skills, difficulty in discerning relevant from irrelevant stimuli, and weak social standing often make it difficult for students with Asperger Syndrome to fully participate in and comprehend unadapted general education curricula and instructional systems. As a result, a number of children and youth with Asperger Syndrome are thought to have learning disabilities (Frith, 1991).

Children and youth with Asperger Syndrome have a neurological disorder. Even though they have the same level of intelligence as other children, the neurological difference impacts how they think, feel, and react. A study at Yale University (Klin, 1999) confirmed this finding. Two groups of

Table 1.1
Asperger Syndrome Definition:
International Classification of Diseases and Related Health Problems–Tenth Edition

A disorder of uncertain nosological validity, characterized by the same kind of qualitative abnormalities of reciprocal social interaction that typify autism, together with a restricted, stereotyped repetitive repertoire of interests and activities. The disorder differs from autism primarily in that there is no general delay or retardation in language or cognitive development. Most individuals are of normal general intelligence but it is common for them to be markedly clumsy; the condition occurs predominantly in boys (in a ratio of about eight boys to one girl). It seems highly likely that at least some cases represent mild varieties of autism, but it is uncertain whether or not that is so for all. There is a strong tendency for abnormalities to persist into adolescence and adult life and it seems that they represent individual characteristics that are not greatly affected by environmental influences. Psychotic episodes occasionally occur in early adult life.

Diagnostic Guidelines

Diagnosis is based on the combination of a lack of any clinically significant general delay in language or cognitive development plus, as with autism, the presence of qualitative deficiencies in restricted, repetitive, stereotyped patterns of behavior, interests, and activities.

There may or may not be problems in communication similar to those associated with autism, but significant language retardation would rule out the diagnosis.

Includes: autistic psychopathy

schizoid disorder of childhood

Excludes: anankastic personality disorder (F60.5)

attachment disorders of childhood (F94.1, F94.2)

obsessive-compulsive disorder (F21)

schizotypal disorder (F21)

simple schizophrenia (F20.6)

Table 1.2
Diagnostic Criteria for
Asperger's Disorder (299.80):
Diagnostic and Statistical Manual
of Mental Disorders–Fourth Edition

A. Qualitative impairment in social interaction, as manifested by at least two of the following:
  (1) marked impairment in the use of multiple nonverbal behaviors such as eye-to-eye gaze, facial expression, body pressure, and gestures to regulate social interaction
  (2) failure to develop peer relationships appropriate to developmental level
  (3) a lack of spontaneous seeking to share enjoyment, interests, or achievements with other people (e.g., by a lack of showing, bringing, or pointing out objects of interest to other people)
  (4) lack of social or emotional reciprocity

B. Restricted repetitive and stereotyped patterns of behavior, interests, and activities, as manifested by at least one of the following:
  (1) encompassing preoccupation with one or more stereotyped and restricted patterns of interest that is abnormal either in intensity or focus
  (2) apparently inflexible adherence to specific, nonfunctional routines or rituals
  (3) stereotyped and repetitive motor mannerisms (e.g., hand or finger flapping or twisting, or complex whole-body movements)
  (4) persistent preoccupation with parts of objects

C. The disturbance causes clinically significant impairment in social, occupational, or other important areas of functioning.

D. There is no clinically significant delay in language (e.g., single words used by age 2 years, communicative phrases used by 3 years).

E. There is no clinically significant delay in cognitive development or in the development of age-appropriate self-help skills, adaptive behavior (other than in social interaction), and curiosity about the environment in childhood.

F. Criteria are not met for another specific Pervasive Developmental Disorder or Schizophrenia.

children were studied: one group had neurological disorders, such as Asperger Syndrome; the other group had no neurological disorders. This study found that when children with neurological disorders were under stress, they reacted emotionally rather than logically. It is as if the "thinking center" of the brain became inactive while the "feeling center" became highly active. Hence, when under stress the individual with Asperger Syndrome reacts and does not think. At this time, the child or youth has a limited ability to place a thought barrier between his impulses and actions. That is, he is less able to inhibit emotional urges. The result is that the child with Asperger Syndrome may engage in rage behavior or blurt out inappropriate phrases because he has limited self-control under stress. It is important to note, however, that when not under stress, children and youth with Asperger Syndrome think and feel as others do.

Generalization

A challenge facing children and youth with Asperger Syndrome relates to their difficulty in generalizing knowledge and skills. That is, they frequently have problems applying information and skills across settings and with different individuals as well as integrating learned material and experience. While students may memorize sets of facts, these lists often remain unconnected bits of information. For example, such students may be able to cite a rule or set of procedures that they are to follow in a given situation, but be incapable of applying them when needed. As a result, teachers often voice concern over this lack of generalization, misinterpreting the lack of symmetry between verbalization and actions as intentional misbehavior.

For example, Fred's typical strategy to engage others in play was to tell his peers what to do. Following even a minor lack of compliance on the part of playmates, Fred would swing at the peer closest to him. Fred's counselor worked with him on developing a strategy to help him cope better when playmates did not engage in the activity the way Fred wanted them to. Fred's strategy was to:

1. Suggest an activity.
2. If his peers indicated an unwillingness to play, he would ask them to play the game again.
3. If the playmates still did not want to engage in Fred's choice of activity, then he would either agree to play another game and suggest his game for next time or tell the peers good-bye and find other children

with the same interests as Fred. Fred verbalized this strategy from cue cards and role-played it in the counselor's office with repeated accuracy. However, when an actual situation occurred on the playground, Fred immediately reverted back to his hitting strategy. The counselor, observing the scene, threw up his hands and said, "Fred must not want to play with the other boys. He knew what he was supposed to do. He just chose not to do it." However, the truth is that Fred was not willingly disobedient, he simply had not generalized the necessary skills beyond verbalization and cued role-play.

This situation is typical of many children with Asperger Syndrome. One explanation for this phenomenon is their neurological immaturity. Two important abilities affect maturity: (a) the ability to retrieve learned behavior from the area of the brain in which it is "filed" for future reference; and (b) the ability to "read," "interpret," and "act" on social clues received from the environment. Both of these abilities are based on using the "thinking" part of the brain, which does not function well under stress in children with Asperger Syndrome and other neurological disabilities. It is no wonder, then, that these children misinterpret social situations and, even with knowledge of how to "act", resort to practiced strategies that they have had in their repertoire for some time.

The analogy of the brain to a computer may help explain the process of how learned behavior is "filed" in the brain and retrieved for later use. When stress affects a child with a neurological disorder, the child is less able to access the "thinking" area of the brain. Therefore, the child does not act in what others perceive to be a logical or rational manner.

This tendency to retrieve established behavioral patterns under stressful circumstances also helps explain why a child may act a certain way even though she has learned better and more acceptable ways of handling a situation. That is, the child may be unable to retrieve a particular newly learned behavior when under stress, yet be capable of recalling it an hour later when not under stress. For example, the parent may say, "What were you thinking about! You knew better! We went over this just last week." And the child will respond, "I don't know–I guess I just was not thinking." (Translation: The child, under stress, did not retrieve the newest learned behavior; instead, previously well-practiced behavior was retrieved.)

Maturity

Maturity is often assessed by actions in social situations. To be socially adept, people must be able to perceive and understand social clues such as frowns, smiles, boredom, emotions, etc. They must be able to think clearly about their own behavior and the behavior of others. They must make sound judgments about the persons around them. All these skills require thinking, and thinking is difficult for the child with neurological difficulties when under stress. As a result, children with these difficulties, such as children with Asperger Syndrome, appear "clueless" or "naive." A rule of thumb: The child with neurological difficulties has an emotional maturity level that is significantly below his/her chronological age. Particularly during the period between ages 9 and 19, children with Asperger Syndrome may appear to have the emotional maturity of someone two-thirds their age.

Rote Memory

Although rote memory may be perceived as an asset, it can be a great detriment for persons with Asperger Syndrome. Because of well-developed rote memory skills, persons with Asperger Syndrome often give the impression that they understand concepts when in fact they do not. Typically, the person with Asperger Syndrome picks up from context or conversation certain words or phrases and uses them in a rote manner that mimics comprehension. Often this parroting gives the impression that the person has well-developed higher-level comprehension skills, whereas comprehension is often actually only at the factual level. That is, persons with Asperger Syndrome can understand basic facts in written material and either repeat them verbatim or paraphrase them. For example, students may be able to repeat the steps to completing a long division problem, but be unable to perform it. Similarly, they may answer multiple-choice questions on a worksheet about a novel they have read, but be unable to understand the main character's motivation.

Rote memory may be a disadvantage for students with Asperger Syndrome in another way. Educators assume that good rote memory means that students can remember, at any time, pieces of information or events. But this is not true for many persons with Asperger Syndrome. While chunks of information are stored in memory, it is often difficult for persons with this exceptionality to determine how to retrieve them. Open-ended questions such as, "Tell me what the main character in the story did after his horse disappeared," may not trigger a response because the student has stored the information under the main character's name and is unable to make the transition from the term "main character" to her actual name.

In students with Asperger Syndrome, therefore, an exceptional memory is not related to the ability to recall information. For example, a friend who has an adult son with Asperger Syndrome met for dinner a young man who was traveling through town. This young man was recently admitted to MIT, a highly competitive university. My friend began polite conversation with the young man by asking him to tell a bit about himself. The MIT admittee made fleeting eye contact and informed my friend that he could not answer open-ended questions. This response came from a person who had passed entrance examinations into MIT–a person who obviously was able to finish high school with a high grade point average and complete MIT entrance examinations with a high skill level.

Theory of Mind Deficits

Persons with Asperger Syndrome are seen to have as one of their core cognitive deficits difficulties with "theory of mind." Some think that it is this deficit that sets children with Asperger Syndrome and autism apart from those with other disabilities (Baron-Cohen, 1988; Baron-Cohen, Allen, & Gillberg, 1992; Baron-Cohen, Jolliffe, Mortimore, & Robertson, 1997; Gath, 1989; Gillberg, 1993; Leslie, 1987; Leslie & Frith, 1988). People with theory of mind problems have difficulty understanding the emotions and mental states of people in social situations. As illustrated below, theory of mind problems have a profound impact on persons with Asperger Syndrome. Those exhibiting difficulties in this area experience the following multitude of academic, behavior, and social problems.

1. Difficulty explaining own behaviors

Even though persons with Asperger Syndrome are highly verbal, they have difficulty explaining why they did something. Even if they have a rationale for engaging in a behavior or social interaction, they often cannot give an adequate explanation.

2. Difficulty understanding emotions

Many students with Asperger Syndrome understand a limited number of emotions. They may only recognize two to three emotions along the continuum from extremely happy to very sad. When they get 100% on a weekly spelling test they are extremely happy. They might exhibit the same degree of emotion when they receive a new bike. There is little understanding of subtleties. Namely, the typical person may be pleased to receive 100% on the test, but be overjoyed to have a new bike.

Not only do persons with Asperger Syndrome have difficulty recognizing the emotions of others, they often have problems understanding their own feelings. They may have difficulty understanding their own state of mind. They may be unable to recognize that they are agitated and that this agitation, unless addressed, may lead to behavior problems.

3. Difficulty predicting the behavior or emotional state of others

Many of our actions and reactions are dictated by how we think others will feel. In school, when a teacher says she is not feeling well, students understand that the teacher may not be as patient as usual and that today is not a good day for practical jokes. Those with Asperger Syndrome do not see this obvious connection between not feeling well and lack of patience. When they pull a practical joke, therefore, they are surprised by the teacher's negative response.

4. Problems understanding the perspectives of others

Teachers often give assignments that require students to assume the role of a historical character, involving writing papers or plays or making a speech as the historical figure. Tasks of this nature are difficult for those who do not understand the human experience from different perspectives. Since persons with Asperger Syndrome have difficulty understanding their own state of mind, they can hardly be expected to be able to imagine the state of mind of others.

5. Problems inferring the intentions of others

Every day, Jorge, a high school student with Asperger Syndrome, walks into the school cafeteria where he is greeted by a group of normally achieving peers. His friends routinely ask, "What's up?" Each day, Jorge looks up to the ceiling to see what is up. The peers laugh. Jorge thinks these boys are his friends. In reality, they are not friends; they are making fun of Jorge.

6. Lack of understanding that behavior impacts how others think and/or feel

Many people with Asperger Syndrome do not make the connection between their actions and others' reactions to them. Jonathan, a young boy with Asperger Syndrome, really wanted to play with Bill on the playground. Jonathan could not understand the relationship between Jonathan's hitting Bill out of anger several times and Bill's unwillingness to associate with him.

7. Problems with joint attention and other social conventions

Persons with Asperger Syndrome have difficulties with turn-taking, perspective-taking, politeness, and numerous other social conventions. Mary, whose passion was earthquakes, would walk up to an individual and begin to spout facts about the latest earthquakes around the world. Further, if someone else attempted to speak with her, she would reply with earthquake statistics. She did not perceive her actions as problematic and a reason why people would turn away.

John was perceived by many of his peers as crazy. His conversation would change course, sometimes in mid-sentence. For example, his first sentence would be about a basketball game score ("Forty-six to 44. Could you believe it?") without reference to team names or even a statement that he was discussing a game. His second sentence would begin with a phrase about the material his t-shirt was made of. In the middle of this sentence, he would make a seemingly random statement about the great taste of jello. He did not understand that the listener could not follow his conversation. To John, his conversation made sense. He was interested in a basketball game he had seen the previous evening, his t-shirt felt "scratchy" and he wanted jello for lunch.

8. Problems differentiating fiction from fact

A young man I know has spent a significant amount of time drawing plans and writing technical reports on how to improve the capability of the Star Trek Enterprise. He sees this vehicle as actually existing and his passion regarding some of the architectural components that he has introduced is often convincing to others who spend time with him. Everyone else knows that the Enterprise is fictional and does not understand the student's inability to understand that it is not reality (Cumine, Leach, & Stevenson, 1998; Jordan & Powell, 1995).

Problem-Solving

While students may be able to engage in high-level thinking and problem-solving when their area of interest is involved, these skills are often not used throughout the school day. Many students with Asperger Syndrome select one problem-solving strategy and use it consistently regardless of the situation or outcome. For example, if the school locker does not open, the student may keep trying the same combination. Although this strategy can be effective, when repeated attempts prove unsuccessful, there needs to be a self-monitoring component. That is, if the student has tried the correct locker combination five times unsuccessfully, chances are that there is another problem with the locker. However, students with Asperger Syndrome might not know the problem-solving strategy that involves asking an adult or peer when difficulty arises and that alternate options are necessary. As a result, persistence, if unsuccessful, can result in inappropriate behavioral outbursts.

Difficulty accessing information or strategies may make problem-solving even more difficult. Although the student may be able to recite several problem-solving strategies and realize that they can be generalized, she may not be able to recall any of these strategies when they are needed. Because the student with Asperger Syndrome often has difficulty searching her memory for particular facts, she may not be able to access that given strategy. Thus, even if the student has an effective system for retrieving problem-solving strategies, it is still likely that she cannot use this system. By the time the student cognitively realizes that a problem exists, she typically is so confused, angry or disoriented that her reaction is behavioral–a tantrum or withdrawal.

Problem-solving becomes even more difficult in academics if abstract concepts are involved. Thus, persons with Asperger Syndrome frequently have difficulty with word problems, estimation, algebra, and geometry, all of which require problem-solving skills and often contain a high level of abstraction.

The deficits of some students with Asperger Syndrome are not easily recognized. Their pedantic style, advanced vocabulary, and grammatically perfect responses often mask their skill levels. Students with this exceptionality often fail to understand what they read despite average to above-average word-calling skills. Teachers, in turn, fail to recognize the special academic needs of students with Asperger Syndrome because these children sound as if they understand more than they do. Students' inability to monitor their own skills also contributes to this problem. As one teacher reported, "Johnny reads much better than my other second graders and can answer many factual questions. It is as if he has memorized key words and phrases and can say them when he is cued. But, he often does this without having an overall understanding of what he has read." Another teacher stated, "Margaret has exceptional rote memory. She reads something once and recalls it verbatim. However, she doesn't know which information to memorize. Margaret memorized the entire list of food and nonfood items brought aboard the Mayflower by the Pilgrims, but did not understand why they had undertaken their journey to America."

Language

Frith (1991) observed that children with Asperger Syndrome "tend to speak fluently by the time they are five, even if their language development was slow to begin with, and even if their language is noticeably odd in its use for communication" (p. 3). Asperger described language onset for children with Asperger Syndrome as occurring at the expected age, while others such as Wing (1981) reported that many individuals with Asperger Syndrome are slow to talk. Wing also noted that many individuals diagnosed with Asperger Syndrome reveal a variety of communication deficits as infants and that many of their perceived "special abilities" may be explained as rote responses rather than normal or precocious language development.

Many children and youth with Asperger Syndrome have good structural language skills, such as clear pronunciation and correct syntax, but poor pragmatic communication abilities. Thus, many use poor language for social interaction and interactive communication. For example, a child may (a) repeat the same phrase over and over, (b) talk with exaggerated inflections or in a monotone and droning style, (c) discuss at length a single topic that is of little interest to others, or (d) experience difficulty in sustaining conversation unless it focuses exclusively on a particular narrowly defined topic. These communication problems are not surprising, given that effective communication requires that individuals have mutually shared topics to communicate about and are willing to listen as well as to talk–common problems for persons with Asperger Syndrome. Moreover, the adult-like and pedantic speaking style of some children and youth with Asperger Syndrome may further lessen their appeal to their peers.

As previously stated, nonverbal communication deficits and related social context communication problems are common among persons with Asperger Syndrome. This includes problems relating to (a) proxemics, or standing closer to or farther away from another person during conversation than is customarily accepted; (b) intensely staring at another person for long periods while interacting; (c) maintaining abnormal body posture in social situations; (d) failing to make eye contact or displaying an inexpressive face, thereby failing to signal interest, approval or disapproval of another person during conversation; and (e) failing to use or understand gestures and facial expressions that accompany verbal messages.

Related to school-based interactions, students with Asperger Syndrome frequently experience difficulty in comprehending language related to describing abstract concepts; understanding and correctly using figures of speech such as metaphors, idioms, parables and allegories; and grasping the meaning and intent of rhetorical questions. A story with a moral of "Don't cry over spilled milk" might be confusing for a student with Asperger Syndrome. She might look for a milk-spilling incident in the story or draw a conclusion that the moral literally means that when milk is spilled, it should just be cleaned up, and people should not cry. Since these conventions are commonly used by authors of school texts and teachers, deficits in this area have a negative impact on the academic success of students with Asperger Syndrome.

Visual Processing

Related to the area of language is visual processing. Although it has been well documented that children and youth with autism process visual information better than auditory information (Quill, 1995), the same type of data does not exist on individuals with Asperger Syndrome. Despite this dearth of evidence, practitioners generally recognize that visually presented information is more easily understood by individuals with this exceptionality. A small but seemingly significant study provides support for the hypothesis that students with Asperger Syndrome process information more easily if it is presented visually. Meara, Brandt, and Myles (in press) found central-auditory processing difficulties in five children and youth with Asperger Syndrome. Although these limited data are not enough on which to base instructional programming, they do support what practitioners have long suspected–to best understand their environment, students with Asperger Syndrome need visual supports.

Socialization

Social relationships in the children Asperger described were a source of conflict early in life. In fact, he reported that one of the hallmark characteristics of these children was an inability to build and maintain social relationships. Asperger posited that the children he studied were often socially isolated because of their seeming lack of interest in what was going on around them, their engagement in stereotypic behaviors, and their tendency to follow their own impulses and interests regardless of others' responses. He also noted that if another individual intruded on the world of a person with this exceptionality, it might prompt an aggressive reaction. Other researchers and practitioners have reported similar social problems related to Asperger Syndrome (Ehlers & Gillberg, 1993; Gath, 1989; Ghaziuddin, Metler, Ghaziuddin, Tsai, & Giordani, 1993; Gillberg & Gillberg, 1989; Szatmari, Bremner, & Nagy, 1989).

Reciprocal social interaction problems found in Asperger Syndrome appear numerous. The inability to interact with peers is marked by (a) lack of understanding of social cues, (b) a tendency to interpret words and/or phrases concretely, and (c) language comprehension problems. In addition, persons with Asperger Syndrome often exhibit a clumsy social style, engage in one-sided social interactions, and have difficulty accurately sensing the feelings of others or taking others' perspective. These children either monopolize or have little to no participation in conversation, show abnormalities in inflection, and repeat phrases inappropriately and out of context.

The social rules considered second nature by many are not innately understood by many persons with Asperger Syndrome. One theory suggests that the impairment in two-way social interaction arises from a lack of ability to understand and use the rules governing social behavior. Individuals with Asperger Syndrome do not know how to initiate and/or maintain a conversation, monitor others' interest in what is being said, use polite verbal and nonverbal cues, or understand such cues given by others. The idea that people may not say what they mean in conversation is also foreign to those with Asperger Syndrome. "Go jump in the lake" may mean to a person with Asperger Syndrome that she is to find a body of water and immerse herself in it. Further, the young man with this exceptionality who is asked "How are you?" may give a lengthy and detailed response about his physical and emotional condition, thinking that the person who asked the question actually is interested in the response.

Individuals with Asperger Syndrome are often seen engaging in simple, routine social interactions such as greetings. However, they are often not able to extend this interaction in a meaningful way. When they do attempt to maintain a conversation, it is often marked by language considered inappropriate. It is as if the filter between the brain and the mouth is not cooperating—they say exactly what comes to mind. This is often called "blurting." "That red dress makes you look fat" or "What you said is stupid" may be uttered by somebody with Asperger Syndrome. There is no intention to hurt or make fun; the person is merely stating something as he sees it. Because of incidents like these, people with Asperger Syndrome are commonly described as lacking an awareness of accepted social protocol and common sense, displaying a propensity to misinterpret social cues and unspoken messages, and being inclined to display a variety of socially unaccepted and nonreciprocal responses.

To many persons with Asperger Syndrome, conversation exists primarily as a means of talking about a topic that is fascinating to them, regardless of audience input or interest. Without the ability to monitor others' thoughts or value the input of others, extensive monologues on a restricted topic often occur. They do not understand that when a person rolls her eyes, crosses her arms, or backs away she is signaling a lack of interest in what is being said.

In spite of their frequent lack of social awareness, many individuals with Asperger Syndrome are aware that they are different from their peers. Thus, self-esteem problems, self-fault finding and self-deprecation are common among individuals with Asperger Syndrome. These problems are exacerbated when the child feels that he cannot control his behavior.

For some of these reasons, children and youth with Asperger Syndrome are poor incidental social learners. That is, they often learn social skills without fully understanding their meaning and context. Sometimes they attempt to rigidly and broadly follow universal social rules, because doing so provides structure to an otherwise confusing world. Unfortunately, this is often not a successful strategy because there are few, if any, universal and inflexible social rules. For example, most middle school students curse. Despite being unable to learn appropriate social skills incidentally, Margery has learned from peers some particularly colorful curse words. She has observed children cursing on the school soccer field and applies the universal rule that cursing is okay outside. She does not, however, learn the nuance that you should not curse when the principal is standing beside you. Consequently, she is thrown into a state of confusion when the principal threatens to punish her for what she considers to be a socially appropriate behavior. Another student, Scott, learns from a peer that it is okay to whisper to peers during seatwork in Mrs. Thompson's class. All students in his class are allowed to ask each other for help and visit as long as it does not hinder assignment completion. But Scott is sent to the office after applying this universal rule in Ms. Swanson's class where the unstated rule and expectation is that no talking is allowed during seatwork. Scott does not understand that different expectations may exist in different settings and that his behavior must change accordingly.

Sensory Issues

Asperger reported that the children and youth he observed were prone to peculiar sensory stimuli responses. For example, children with Asperger Syndrome are often hypersensitive to certain sounds or visual stimuli, such as fluorescent lights, and may respond negatively when overloaded with certain types of sensory stimuli. Parents and teachers have reported behavior problems associated with these children's fear of anticipated unpleasant sensory stimuli such as city whistle signals, chimes or fire alarms that are sounded at certain times. Additionally, it is common for parents of children with Asperger Syndrome to report that these children have a strong and obsessive preference for certain foods and textures (e.g., child will only wear clothes made of certain fabrics or cannot tolerate clothing tags touching skin); and some individuals with Asperger Syndrome have been found to have an extremely high tolerance for physical pain. Other parents of children with Asperger Syndrome have related problems with their children getting their socks to fit "just right" so that the toe seam does not rub their feet.

Reports on sensory problems for persons with Asperger Syndrome are largely anecdotal. However, a preliminary descriptive study appears to support parent observations and the contentions of persons with Asperger

Syndrome themselves. Orr, Myles and Dunn (1999) found that parents and educators of children and youth with Asperger Syndrome noted that the following sensory behaviors were frequently observed in their children and students: (a) is distracted or has trouble focusing in the presence of varied stimuli; (b) prefers quiet, sedentary games; (c) has difficulty paying attention; (d) prefers certain tastes; (e) has difficulty tolerating changes in plans and expectations; (f) exhibits low frustration tolerance; and (g) seems anxious. Similarly, in the norming of a survey to identify children as having Asperger Syndrome, sensory items on the checklist failed to differentiate children with Asperger Syndrome from those with autism. That is, both groups displayed a similar profile (Myles, Simpson, & Bock, 1999).

Behavior

While behavioral problems are not universal among students with Asperger Syndrome, they are not uncommon. When behavioral difficulties do occur, they typically appear to be a function of (a) social ineptness, (b) lack of understanding, (c) a high stress level, (d) lack of control over the environment, (e) an obsessive and single-minded pursuit of a certain interest, or (f) a defensive panic reaction. Thus, the behavior problems of children with Asperger Syndrome are connected to their more generalized inability to function in a world they perceive to be unpredictable and threatening. Thus, there appears to be little support for Asperger's original description of children with Asperger Syndrome as malicious and mean-spirited.

On the behavioral continuum, children and youth with Asperger Syndrome may range from withdrawn to active. Regardless of where they fall on this continuum, however, they are routinely viewed as socially awkward and stiff, emotionally blunted, self-centered, unable to understand nonverbal social cues, inflexible, and lacking in empathy and understanding. Therefore, even when children and adolescents with Asperger Syndrome actively seek out others, they usually encounter social isolation because of their lack of understanding of the rules of social behavior, including eye contact, proximity to others, gestures, posture, and so forth.

Stress and Excitement

It is also common for individuals with Asperger Syndrome to become emotionally vulnerable and easily stressed. In fact, some argue that persons with Asperger Syndrome are under constant or near-constant stress. Wanting to play with another child and not knowing how, trying to follow teacher directions but not understanding what is being said, hearing children laugh around you and not getting the joke–these are all stressful situations that children and youth with Asperger Syndrome experience daily.

Children with Asperger Syndrome may become agitated by something as simple as perceiving others as invading their private space in the lunch line or when they find themselves in the midst of several simultaneous social activities. However, unlike many normally developing and achieving peers, many children with Asperger Syndrome do not reveal their stress through voice tone, body posture, and so forth. As a result, their agitation often escalates to a point of crisis because of others' unawareness of their discomfort, along with their own inability to monitor and control uncomfortable situations. Further, their behaviors are often exacerbated by fatigue.

Excitement often causes the same reaction as stress. Many parents report that they cannot tell their child with Asperger Syndrome in advance of a highly favored activity. The child, in anticipation, becomes overexcited, cannot monitor his behavior, and loses control. Many households have forbidden their children to "horse around", that age-old game where children playfully touch each other and wrestle. Children with Asperger Syndrome often become engrossed in horse play and cannot control their level of interaction with a peer.

Given these deficits, it is not surprising that children and youth with Asperger Syndrome are relatively easy targets for peers prone to teasing and bullying. One young man with Asperger Syndrome, Mark, was almost always near crisis. Rigid in how he thought other high school students should behave, he carried around the school code of conduct book and when he saw an infraction (i.e., someone cursing), he would approach the offending party and recite the rule that was being broken and even the page number where the offense appeared in the manual. Many students did not appreciate Mark's law-abiding behavior. One day when several boys were smoking outside of school in front of Mark, he became extremely anxious, citing that the school did not allow students to smoke. The students told Mark that the code book he had was out-of-date and that a new book had been printed that did allow smoking. Mark became even more anxious in his attempt to explain that his manual was current. Unable to convince the students that they were not supposed to smoke, he reverted to screaming.

Distractibility and Inattention

Many persons with Asperger Syndrome have an attention deficit/hyperactive disorder (ADHD) diagnosis at one time in their lives (Myles, Simpson, & Becker, 1994-1995). Indeed, Asperger Syndrome and ADHD share many commonalities, particularly in terms of distractibility and inattentiveness. Attention often seems fleeting. One moment, the student with Asperger Syndrome may appear to be attending, the next moment he suddenly seems to withdraw into an inner world and be totally unaware of the environment. Teacher directions are not processed; student conversations are not heard. This daydreaming may occur over extended time periods, with no predictability. The daydreaming is often so intense that a physical prompt from the teacher is needed to call the student back to task. Often the antecedent is unknown, but it may be related to stress, focus on an obsessive interest, or overstimulation.

Even while attending, the student may not react to teacher instructions. For example, the student may start to follow a three-step direction, but appear to lose focus as she completes the first phase. Rather than looking for a model or asking for help, she will look for a way out. The student may remain frozen in the same place, wander aimlessly about, shuffle through her desk, stare into space, or begin to daydream. On rare occasions, the student may cause a distraction or act out. Often these same behaviors are evidenced when the student is required to engage in nonpreferred work tasks for extended periods.

Social interactions are often distracting for persons with Asperger Syndrome. Because they want to interact with others, they tend to focus all their attention on others in the classroom instead of on the tasks at hand. If the student with Asperger Syndrome has a particularly strong need to interact with a specific classmate, he may attend to that person exclusively, staring nonstop at the targeted individual or listening in on that person's conversations. If the person with Asperger Syndrome and his classmate have developed a reciprocal relationship, the person with Asperger Syndrome might unilaterally seek that person's approval before beginning a task or addressing the teacher or another student. This gives the peer an enormous amount of power over the person with Asperger Syndrome. For example, the peer may prompt the student with Asperger Syndrome to complete assignments for her, ask the student to break classroom rules or prompt the student to engage in activities that will place the person with Asperger Syndrome in jeopardy.

Distractions may also occur because students with Asperger Syndrome do not know how to determine relevant from irrelevant stimuli. For example, the student with Asperger Syndrome may focus on a particular picture or map in a textbook while other students in the class have moved on to the next chapter or she may focus on the way a speaker's earring dangles when she moves her head instead of listening to the content of her lecture. At this time, the student may seem to have a "laser-like" focus on a particular object. A high level of frustration may occur when the student with Asperger Syndrome attempts to memorize every fact associated with a particular World War II battle mentioned in the text, including an extensive list of weaponry. The student does not innately know that memorizing such information is not necessary.

Tunnel Vision

School requires that students attend to certain stimuli while screening out irrelevant, yet competing distractors. That is, at any given time a student might be expected to attend to a textbook and ignore (a) students talking around her, (b) a teacher offering another student help, and (c) a bulletin board that overviews a favored topic. This is often difficult for the student with Asperger Syndrome for several reasons.

Tunnel vision impairs the student's ability to discern relevant from irrelevant information. If the bulletin board contains information on a topic of high interest, the student may consider it more important than a text. If a student with Asperger Syndrome has a strong social attachment to someone across the room, interacting with that person might take precedence over any task the teacher assigned. Rational explanations that talking across the room is inappropriate may not impact the student with Asperger Syndrome, who might seem "driven" to interact with his friend.

Tunnel vision also impacts logical thinking and flexibility. Students with Asperger Syndrome logically group items or characteristics so that they can make sense of them. That is, they form a schema that is exact and often inflexible. For example, a student who learns the spelling rule, "I before E except after C," might apply the rule rigidly. The student would then be convinced that words like *neighbor* and *weigh* should be spelled *nieghbor* and *wiegh*, respectively.

Problems can present themselves when the student is reading for information, such as reading from a social studies text to answer questions on a worksheet. Generally, reading for information is a difficult task. Students with Asperger Syndrome most likely will read to find specific text information presented on a worksheet or study guide and ignore and not process in a meaningful way information that they were not responsible for knowing. When the student is later tested and given questions that were not on the study guide, the student most likely will not answer those questions or answer them incorrectly, even if the information seems obvious to others.

Obsessions are another hallmark of tunnel vision. Two types of obsessions are generally exhibited by persons with Asperger Syndrome. In the first type of obsession (primary), the student's level of interest is all-encompassing. As a result, a discussion of the topic of interest can escalate to almost tantrum-like behavior, where the student cannot control his discussion of the topic and behavior. Rapid speech, increased volume, a high-pitched voice, pacing, and hand wringing often occur with primary obsessions. Primary obsessions typically do not lend themselves to rational discussions and explorations (Myles & Simpson, 1998). That is, students cannot be talked out of them. Secondary obsessions, on the other hand, refer to marked student interests wherein the student remains lucid, focused, and ready to learn about a particular topic. Students actively seek new information about the topic, but can be somewhat easily redirected. Often secondary interests are used by teachers to motivate students to complete academic tasks. Temple Grandin (1999), an adult with Asperger Syndrome, suggests that secondary interests may be developed into career choices.

Structure, Organization, and Flexibility

Students with Asperger Syndrome typically fall at the ends of the continuum of structure: they either have an inherent ability to provide structure or they totally rely on others to help them organize themselves. As a result, it is often said that students with Asperger Syndrome have either the neatest or the messiest desks in class.

Nevertheless, it is generally easier for persons with Asperger Syndrome to function in an organized environment. Predictable schedules, uniform assignment formats, and consistent teacher affect help these students devote their time and energy to academic tasks. Those who have internal structure tend to hold rigid expectations that schedules be followed and commitments be honored without fail. As a result, unscheduled events cause these student great discomfort, which can be manifested as disorientation, refusal to engage in the new activity, extended discourse about the canceled or post-poned event, or behavior problems. In other words, the student communi-cates through language and behavior that change is difficult.

Educators comment that they have seen a student with Asperger Syndrome tolerate change in some instances, but have evidenced other situ-ations when the student lost control when the environment was altered. Sometimes students with Asperger Syndrome can tolerate change, if that change occurs in only one dimension. For example, if library time is changed the student may adjust to the new schedule. However, if library time and the librarian change simultaneously, the same student may have difficulty maintaining any type of self-control.

Most students with Asperger Syndrome have a limited ability to structure their own environment. A messy person with Asperger Syndrome probably has not made a conscious choice to be that way; rather, he lacks good orga-nizational skills. The student with this disability can literally lose a paper received only one minute earlier. He never has a pencil in class. The note that the teacher placed in the student's backpack never makes it home. Written work is not placed in a uniform manner on a page. The middle school student's locker is a mess; often he cannot locate his locker combina-tion and when he does, he cannot find what he needs to get in his locker. He cannot organize his day by bringing both his science and his math book to science class even though his math class follows immediately afterwards in the room next door. Almost every facet of the student's life is in disarray.

Teachers and parents often wonder how the student with Asperger Syndrome gets from one place to another. It is a challenge to organize this type of student. Merely providing a schedule or list of supplies is not enough. These aids are most often lost so teachers must (a) help students learn organizational skills, (b) minimize loss of visual supports by velcroing them inside books or lockers, and (c) have additional copies of visual sup-ports on hand when the student needs them.

Summary

The challenges and assets associated with Asperger Syndrome are many and varied. The areas of (a) cognition, (b) language, (c) socialization, (c) sensory issues, (d) visual processing, and (e) behavior each presents with symptoms that differentiate these individuals from normally achieving chil-dren. Sometimes when the environment is structured in such a way that persons with Asperger Syndrome can't have their needs met or don't understand behavioral, social, or academic expectations, an unfortunate event will occur–a rage attack, behavioral outburst or tantrum. Regardless of what name it is known by, such a reaction is debilitating to the person with Asperger Syndrome and those around her. The following chapter discusses the phenomenon we call *rage*.

Throughout this book, we use the terms *rage, meltdowns, neurological storms,* and *tantrums* interchangeably to describe behavioral outbursts. Please note that these terms may also describe intense behaviors that may be internalized. Some children and youth turn these extreme behaviors inward.

The Rage Cycle
and Functional Assessment
of Behaviors in the Cycle

Many students with Asperger Syndrome view school as a stressful environment, presenting several stressors that are ongoing and of great magnitude. Stressors include difficulty predicting events because of changing schedules, tuning in to and understanding teacher directions, and interacting with peers. Students with this exceptionality rarely indicate in any meaningful way that they are under stress or experiencing difficulty coping. In fact, they may not always know that they are near a stage of crisis. Quite often they just "tune out" or daydream or state in a monotone voice a seemingly benign phrase, such as "I don't know what to do." Since no emotion is conveyed, these behaviors often go unnoticed by teachers. Then at a later point in time, the student engages, seemingly without provocation, in a verbally or physically aggressive event, often called a rage attack, meltdown or neurological storm. The student may begin to scream or kick over a desk. There seems to be no predictability to this behavior; it just occurs.

Other students with Asperger Syndrome do not display these types of behaviors in school. Sometimes teachers report that the student with Asperger Syndrome is doing fine or managing in school in spite of academic and social problems. However, parents report that when their children arrive home, they often lose control. That is, the child experiences the rage attack, meltdown or neurological storm at home. It seems as if these students have used all of their self-control to manage at school, and once they get to a safe environment, they let go of some of the pressure that is bottled up within them. Thus, rage attacks can occur either at home or school.

Although it may seem that way, rage attacks do not occur without warning. Rather, students with Asperger Syndrome exhibit a pattern of behaviors that are precursors to a behavioral outburst. Sometimes these behaviors are subtle. In fact, those who do not know the student often report that a rage attack comes out of nowhere. One teacher reported, "Susan was just sitting at her desk quietly. The next thing I know, she had a meltdown. She totally lost control, overturned her desk and began flailing her arms. I had no warning." Without a clear understanding of rage and the cycle in which it occurs, it may indeed appear as if rage occurs without warning. This chapter explains the rage cycle and functional analysis, a means of determining why behaviors occur.

The Rage Cycle

Rage occurs for a reason—underlying causes or antecedents serve as triggers. Intervention at early stages often prevents rage attacks. Rage attacks typically run through a course of three stages. These stages can be of variable length, with one stage lasting hours and another only minutes. These stages are (a) the rumbling stage, (b) the rage stage, and (c) the recovery stage (adapted from Albert, 1989; Beck, 1985).

The Rumbling Stage

During the rumbling stage, students with Asperger Syndrome exhibit specific behavioral changes that may not appear to be directly related to a rage attack. Students may bite their nails or lips, lower their voices, tense their muscles, tap their foot, grimace, or otherwise indicate general discontent. Students may also complain of not feeling well. It is easy at this stage to ignore these seemingly minor behaviors; yet, these behaviors often indicate an impending crisis. Students may also engage in behaviors that are more pronounced, including withdrawing from others, either emotionally or physically, or lashing out at or threatening the teacher or other students, either verbally or physically. The student may challenge the classroom structure or authority by attempting to engage in a power struggle.

During this stage, it is imperative that the teacher intervene with the student without becoming part of a struggle. Teacher interventions during this stage often fall under the realm of surface behavior management (Long, Morse & Newman, 1976). That is, teachers can use a variety of strategies such as antiseptic bouncing, proximity control, signal interference or touch control to stop future behavior problems. Each of these strategies will be briefly discussed below.

Antiseptic Bouncing

Antiseptic bouncing involves removing a student, in a nonpunitive fashion, from the environment in which she is experiencing difficulty. For example, Keisha is asked to take a note to the teacher across the hall. Jerome is asked to go to the art area to clean up supplies. Andy, who is asked to deliver the lunch count to the office, typically does not go directly from his classroom to the office. Rather, he stops by the water fountain, wanders by the class of a friend, stops to say hello to the custodian, and then gets to the office. The way back to the classroom is equally circuitous. During this time, the student has had an opportunity to regain a sense of calm. When he returns to the classroom, the problem has typically diminished in magnitude and the teacher is on hand for support if needed.

Proximity Control

Rather than calling attention to the behavior, using this strategy the teacher moves near the student who is engaged in the target behavior. Often something as simple as standing next to a student can be calming. This can be easily accomplished without interrupting the lesson. The teacher who circulates through the classroom during a lesson is using proximity control.

Signal Interference

When the student begins to exhibit a seemingly minor precursor behavior, the teacher uses a nonverbal signal to let the student know that she is aware of the situation. For example, the teacher can place herself in a position where eye contact with the student can be achieved. Or a "secret" signal between teacher and the student can be used as a warning to watch the problem behavior. Many teachers snap their fingers, flick a light switch, or look away to indicate that inappropriate behavior is occurring. Some of these techniques can be used to prevent problem behaviors from occurring.

Touch Control

Sometimes a touch can serve to stop behavior. Gently touching the foot or leg of a student who is tapping his feet loudly may stop disruptive behavior.

Defusing Tension Through Humor

This technique involves using a joke or humorous remark in a potentially tense or potentially eruptive moment. A joke can often prevent group contagion from occurring and salvage an interrupted lesson. Care must be taken to ensure that the student understands the humor and does not perceive herself as the target of a joke.

Support from Routine

Displaying a chart or visual schedule of expectations and events can provide security to students. This technique can also be used as advance preparation for a change in routine. Informing students of schedule alterations can prevent anxiety and save the teacher and class from disruption. The student who is signaling frustration by tapping his foot may be directed to his schedule to make him aware that after he completes two more problems he gets to work on a topic of special interest with a peer.

Interest Boosting

Sometimes showing a personal interest in a student and her hobbies can assist a student in acting appropriately. This involves (a) making the student aware that you recognize her individual preferences or (b) structuring lessons around a topic of interest. Interest boosting can often stop or prevent off-task or acting-out behavior.

The aforementioned strategies can be effective in stopping the rage cycle. They are invaluable in that they can help the student regain control without stopping class routine or calling undue attention to the student.

Other strategies exist that do not fall under the category of surface management but are similar in that they are therapeutic, nonpunitive, and designed to support student success. These include redirecting, home base, and acknowledging student difficulties.

Redirecting

Redirecting involves helping the student to focus on something other than the task at hand. One type of redirection that often works well when the source of the problem behavior is a lack of understanding is telling the student that he and you can cartoon the situation in order to figure out what to do. Sometimes the student can "pull it together" until cartooning (see Chapter 3) can be done at a later time; at other times, the student may need to cartoon immediately.

Home Base

Teachers can create a safe home base for students with Asperger Syndrome. This is a place where students can go when they feel a need to regain control. Resource rooms or counselors' offices can be safe places. One student we know uses the custodian's office as his home base. When students feel the need to leave the classroom, they can take assignments to the home base and work on them there in a less stressful environment. For some students it is helpful to schedule their days so that they begin at the home base and then have frequent stops in this same location. In this way, students have a teacher with whom they have a consistent and constant relationship as well as a place to retreat to when the need arises (Myles & Simpson, 1998).

Acknowledging Student Difficulties

When the student is in the middle of the rumbling stage, the teacher should state the rule to which the student should adhere universally and back it up through personalization and proximity. That is, the teacher should clearly state the rule along with the student's name, indicating that "everyone in the class follows the rule." Although face-to-face contact is not recommended, close distance when communicating a rule and direct eye contact intensify the power of the message. Under no circumstances should the teacher engage in lengthy conversation about "who is right" or "who is in control" (Valentine, 1987). This will only encourage escalation of the target behavior. For example, when working on a math problem the student begins to say, "This is too hard." The teacher, knowing the student can complete the problem, refocuses the student's attention by saying, "Yes, the problem is difficult. Please do number one." Often, just such an acknowledgment and a brief direction prevents the student from getting stuck in the rumbling stage.

In another situation, the teacher might say, "John, when it is difficult to finish work, we use the home base to help students stay on track. Please take your work to your home base." He may then take an icon that says home base and place it on John's desk. In yet another scenario, the teacher might state, "You can play with the ball until the timer sounds, then it is Marvin's turn. In this class, we all take turns." At this critical juncture, the teacher might want to reinforce his verbalizations with an icon. The teacher uses a calm, but firm voice and does not move in a manner that could seem threatening.

Just Walk and Don't Talk

Sometimes an effective strategy is to walk with the student, if the student is not a "runner." Typically, the adult should walk with the student without talking, because during the rumbling stage, anything the adult says will be the wrong thing. The child is not thinking logically and will most likely react emotively to any adult statement, misinterpreting it or rephrasing it in such a way that its original intent is not recognizable. On this walk the child can say whatever she wishes without fear of discipline or logical argument. The adult should be calm, show as little reaction as possible, and never be confrontational.

When selecting a technique during the rumbling stage, it is important to know the student, as the wrong technique can escalate rather than de-escalate a behavior problem. For example, touch control for some students with Asperger Syndrome appears to drain off frustration. That is, by merely touching the student's shoulder, the teacher can feel an immediate relaxation on the part of the student. But another student might be startled by a touch from the teacher because he (a) did not know the teacher was going to enter his space, (b) misperceived touch as an aggression, or (c) perceived touch as discomforting or painful. In these cases, touch control would have the opposite effect of the one intended.

Interventions at this stage do not require extensive teacher time, but it is wise to understand the events that precipitate the target behaviors so that teachers can (a) be ready to intervene early or (b) teach students strategies to maintain behavioral control during these times. However, it is important to understand that interventions at this stage are merely band-aids. They do not teach students to recognize their own frustration or provide a means of handling it. Techniques to accomplish these goals will be discussed later on in the book.

Just as it is important to understand interventions that may diffuse a crisis, it is imperative that educators know which teacher behaviors are likely to escalate behavior problems. Albert (1989) provides a list of behaviors that are almost certain to turn a potential crisis into a rage attack (see Table 2.1).

Rage Stage

If student behavior is not diffused during the rumbling stage, a rage attack, meltdown or neurological storm may occur. At this point, the student is disinhibited and acts impulsively, emotionally, and sometimes explosively. These behaviors may include screaming, biting, hitting, kicking, destroying property or self-injury.

During this stage, another type of rage may also manifest itself, internal rage. The student may become so upset that she completely withdraws, unable to verbalize or act in a rational manner. Emphasis should be placed on student, peer, and teacher safety as well as protection of school, home, or personal property. The best way to cope with the rage attack is to get the child to a safe room. This may be the room in which the behavior occurs, devoid of materials that can be destroyed and of other children who may unintentionally be harmed. The room is equipped with objects that help the child calm down and relax. The room is not viewed as a reward or disciplinary room, but is seen as a place where the student can regain self-control.

Rage attacks are not purposeful, and once the rage stage begins, it most often must run its course. Adams (1997) related a rage incident in a young boy, "The first rage attack for one young man occurred while in a parking lot. A stranger swore at him and called him a 'stupid kid.' The boy started to shake a mailbox, and began to kick and scream. ... It was noted by the parent that during later attacks, the boy would sometimes say, 'I don't want to do this!' It appeared that he could not disengage from the emotion, once it had started" (p. 72).

Importance should be placed on helping the student regain control and preserving her dignity. Teachers should have developed plans for (a) obtaining assistance from educators such as a crisis teacher or principal, (b) removing other students from the area, or (c) providing therapeutic restraint, if necessary.

Table 2.1
Teacher Behaviors That Escalate a Crisis

Raising voice	Making assumptions
Yelling	Backing the student into a corner
Saying "I'm the boss here"	Pleading or bribing
Insisting on having the last word	Bringing up unrelated events
Using tense body language, such as rigid posture and clenched hands	Generalizing by making remarks such as "You kids are all the same"
Preaching	Making unsubstantiated accusations
Using sarcasm	Holding a grudge
Attacking the student's character	Nagging
Acting superior	Throwing a temper tantrum
Using unwarranted physical force	Mimicking the student
Drawing unrelated persons into the conflict	Making comparisons with siblings, other students, etc.
Having a double standard: "Do what I say, not what I do"	Commanding, demanding, dominating
Insisting that the teacher is right	Rewarding the student for unacceptable behavior or for decreasing rage behavior
Using degrading, insulting, humiliating or embarrassing putdowns	

Adapted from: Albert, L. (1989). *A teacher's guide to cooperative discipline: How to manage your classroom and promote self-esteem.* Circle Pines, MN: American Guidance Service.

Recovery Stage

Although many believe that the crisis cycle ends with rage, this is not the case. There is also a third stage: the recovery stage. Following the rage attack, the child has contrite feelings and often cannot fully remember the rage attack. He may become sullen, withdraw, or deny that inappropriate behavior occurred. Some children are so physically exhausted after a rage attack that they need to sleep.

It is imperative that appropriate interventions are implemented at a time when they can be accepted by the student and in a manner that the student understands. If appropriate interventions are not implemented at this point, the result is most often another rage attack or meltdown. In addition, teachers should plan ahead whether this time should also be used for instruction, interpretation, and modification of the student's environment. Often at this stage, the child is not ready to learn. Thus, it is important that teachers work with students to help them to once again become a part of the classroom routine. This if often best accomplished by directing the student to a highly motivating task that he can easily accomplish.

Functional Assessment of Behavior

Each student displays unique behaviors throughout the crisis cycle. Understanding behaviors at each stage helps teachers or parents plan interventions that can prevent or de-escalate a potential rage attack. As mentioned earlier, student behaviors typically do not occur in isolation or randomly; they are most often associated with a reason or cause. The student who engages in an inappropriate behavior is attempting to communicate. Before selecting interventions that might be effective during the rage cycle, it is important to understand the function or role the behavior plays. Functional assessment provides a means of determining the conditions under which behaviors in the rage cycle occur. As such, it is a first step in developing effective interventions. Indeed, without determining reasons, causes, or conditions under which a behavior occurs, it is unlikely that an intervention will be effective. The following six steps comprise a functional assessment:

- identify and describe student behavior
- describe setting demands and antecedents
- collect baseline data and/or work samples
- complete functional analysis measures and develop a hypothesis
- develop and implement a behavioral intervention plan
- collect data and follow up to analyze the effectiveness of the plan

Identify and Describe Student Behavior

Most basic to the process of functional assessment is identifying and describing the behavior on which the intervention is to be structured. When examining the student's role in the rage cycle, it is important to clearly operationalize the behavior or behaviors that are evident. Behaviors are stated in observable terms so that everyone who comes in contact with the child recognizes the same behaviors. If, on the other hand, student behaviors are amorphously defined, it is likely that not all educators will recognize the behavior and, thus, they will not apply designated interventions at the appropriate time. A behavior identified as "the student shows stress," for example, does little to help the fourth-grade teacher understand when the student with Asperger Syndrome is entering the rage cycle. Behaviors should be described as verbs with information on how it is performed, how often it occurs, duration, and intensity. The teacher who observes "the student under stress begins to pace rapidly back and forth while whispering" can easily recognize the behavior.

Describe Setting Demands and Antecedents

Before designing an intervention, it is important to have an understanding of the environment(s) in which the behaviors are likely to occur. The Autism Asperger Resource Center (1997) designed a checklist that helps describe the classroom environment by asking specific questions regarding (a) teaching methods, (b) grading, (c) tests, (d) teaching materials, (e) product requirements, (f) student behavior, (g) class management, and (h) class structure. All of these components are integral in understanding why a behavior may be occurring (see Figure 2.1).

Other factors related to setting demands include time factors, instructional expectations, behavioral expectations, and social demands.

Collect Baseline Data and/or Work Samples

Concurrent with describing setting demands and antecedents is observation of the student in environments in which the targeted behavior does and does not occur. Observation data, an important component of the functional assessment process, should be collected to document behavior frequency, duration, and/or intensity (Kerr & Nelson, 1993). Again, it is extremely important that behavioral data be collected both in the environments where the behavior occurs and where it does not occur. Permanent products or work samples should also be analyzed to determine student achievement rate across academic settings.

Assessing the Setting Demands in the Classroom

Name: _____ Class: _____ Date: _____

Please complete this questionnaire to help us support instruction in your class.
Circle the number that best answers each question.

TEACHING METHODS	Never	Sometimes	Always

A. % of class time spent in lecture . . . . _____%

B. % of class time spent in discussion . . . . _____%

C. % of learning done through
   independent study . . . . _____%

D. % of time in cooperative
   learning groups . . . . _____%

	Never		Sometimes		Always
E. Is there a consistent daily routine?	1	2	3	4	5
F. Is there a consistent weekly routine?	1	2	3	4	5

COMMENTS: _____

_____

GRADES	Never		Sometimes		Always
A. Is extra credit work accepted and/or encouraged?	1	2	3	4	5
B. Can students rework previous assignments?	1	2	3	4	5
C. Is the grading criteria established and posted at the beginning of the course?	1	2	3	4	5

COMMENTS: _____

_____

TESTS	Never		Sometimes		Always
A. Is a variety of test methods used in your class?	1	2	3	4	5
1. Multiple-choice tests?	1	2	3	4	5
2. Essay tests?	1	2	3	4	5
3. Matching tests?	1	2	3	4	5
4. True/false tests?	1	2	3	4	5
5. Open book tests?	1	2	3	4	5
6. Take-home tests?	1	2	3	4	5
7. Group/cooperative tests?	1	2	3	4	5
B. Are tests given in your class?	1	2	3	4	5
1. Daily tests?	1	2	3	4	5
2. Weekly tests?	1	2	3	4	5
3. Monthly tests?	1	2	3	4	5
4. Quarterly tests?	1	2	3	4	5
C. Do you allow test taking assistance for students?	1	2	3	4	5

COMMENTS: _____

_____

Figure 2.1. Setting demands checklist.

TEACHING MATERIALS	Never		Sometimes		Always
A. Do you use a textbook?............................ 1		2	3	4	5
B. Do you use handouts?............................ 1		2	3	4	5
C. Do students need to bring outside materials to class? . . 1		2	3	4	5
List materials needed: _____					
D. Are prerequisite skills required? 1		2	3	4	5
List skills: _____					
E. Are typing/word processing skills required? 1		2	3	4	5

COMMENTS: _____

_____

WRITTEN & OTHER MAJOR PRODUCTS	Never		Sometimes		Always
A. Are students required to write in complete sentences? . . 1		2	3	4	5
B. Are students required to write paragraphs?........... 1		2	3	4	5
C. Are students required to write essays or					
3-5 paragraphs?................................. 1		2	3	4	5
D. Is a research paper required? 1		2	3	4	5
E. Is an oral presentation required? 1		2	3	4	5
F. Are there any required major course					
projects/assignments?............................ 1		2	3	4	5
List: _____					
G. How often do you require students to answer					
questions in written form? 1		2	3	4	5

COMMENTS: _____

_____

STUDENT BEHAVIOR	Never		Sometimes		Always
A. Is on-time behavior factored into the grade?.......... 1		2	3	4	5
B. Is attendance factored into the grade? 1		2	3	4	5
C. Is student participation factored into the grade?....... 1		2	3	4	5
D. Is work completion factored into the grade? 1		2	3	4	5
E. Are other student behaviors factored into the grade? . . . 1		2	3	4	5
List behaviors (i.e., on-task behavior, listening, etc.): _____					
F. Is student notetaking an important part of your class? . . 1		2	3	4	5
G. Are students expected to manage their out-of-class					
behavior independently?.......................... 1		2	3	4	5

COMMENTS: _____

_____

Figure 2.1. Continued

CLASS MANAGEMENT Never Sometimes Always
A. Are rules and guidelines posted and
reviewed in your classroom?. 1 2 3 4 5
B. Are consequences clearly communicated to the students?. 1 2 3 4 5
C. Do you use material reinforcements?. 1 2 3 4 5
D. Do you use other reinforcements? 1 2 3 4 5
List: _____

COMMENTS: _____

_____

CLASSROOM STRUCTURE Never Sometimes Always
A. What is your present classroom seating arrangement?
Draw a quick picture.

Example   Your room

T
S S S S S
S S S S S
S S S S S

B. How often are students in the above
seating arrangements?. 1 2 3 4 5
C. What other alternate arrangements do you use?

Draw a quick picture.

D. How often are students in the above alternate
seating arrangements? 1 2 3 4 5
COMMENTS: _____

_____

Figure 2.1. Continued

Used with the permission of the Autism Asperger Resource Center, 3901 Rainbow Blvd., Kansas City, KS 66160-7335, 913/588-5988, fax 913/588-5942 (www.KUMC.edu/AARC).

Complete Functional Analysis Measures and Develop a Hypothesis

To most effectively and efficiently intervene with a problem behavior, it is important to understand the cause, triggers, or functions of that behavior. The goal of functional assessment and related intervention procedures is not simply to eradicate a behavior, but to help the student learn new and more appropriate ways of having his needs met. Researchers and practitioners have developed a list of possible behavior functions or triggers that include (a) escape/avoidance; (b) attention from peers or adults; (c) anger or stress expression; (d) emotional state, such as depression, frustration or confusion; (e) power/control; (f) intimidation; (g) sensory stimulation; (h) fear or relief of fear; (i) request to obtain something (i.e., food, activity, object, comfort, routine, social interaction); or (j) expression of internal stimulation (i.e., sinus pain, skin irritation, hunger). Other triggers for children with Asperger Syndrome may include (a) obsessional thoughts, (b) fear of failure, (c) fear related to self-esteem (i.e., loss of face, loss of perceived position), or (d) the need to protect an irrational thought. Understanding which of these functions the behavior serves is one of the initial steps in setting up an effective intervention.

Several commercial functional assessment instruments are available to help teachers and parents identify behavior functions or triggers (i.e., *Motivation Assessment Scale*, Durand & Crimmins, 1992; *Student-Assisted Functional-Assessment Interview*, Kern, Dunlap, Clarke, & Childs, 1994; *Problem Behavior Questionnaire*, Lewis, Scott & Sugai, 1994; *Functional Assessment Interview Form*, O'Neill, Horner, Albin, Sprague, Storey & Newton, 1997) (see Figure 2.2 for sample copies of some of these instruments).

Many school districts, instead of relying on instruments that are not tailor-made for their school environment and culture, have created tools that are effective in identifying behavior function. McConnell, Hilvitz, and Cox (1998), for example, developed for their school district a functional assessment and data collection packet (see Figure 2.3).

Develop and Implement a Behavioral Intervention Plan

Once functional assessment data have been collected, reviewed and analyzed, the information should be assimilated to gain a thorough understanding of the rage cycle. This process is important because the cycle most often reveals a pattern and, therefore, provides important information for future interventions. The typical pattern of a rage attack is:

1. Each storm has a build-up.
2. Each episode is preceded by a trigger or set of triggers.
3. The build-up to the rage attack, meltdown, or neurological storm is typically manifested in the same way.
4. Each episode lasts approximately the same length of time.

Once the analysis has occurred and each of these four issues have been defined, it is time to write a behavioral intervention plan. In accordance with the reauthorization of the Individuals with Disabilities Education Act (1997), this plan includes a written description of specific interventions to use with the student to promote behavioral, social, and academic success. In addition, persons who will be responsible for implementation of the plan must be delineated.

As an accompaniment to a behavioral intervention plan, the *Student Crisis Plan Sheet* (see Figure 2.4) can be a useful tool in specifically outlining student behaviors and needed interventions for each stage in the rage cycle. This form helps educators and parents (a) develop a blueprint of events that are likely to precipitate rage, (b) identify behaviors the student exhibits at each stage of the rage cycle, and (c) outline interventions that can be used at each stage to help the student regain behavioral control. The form is also helpful in ensuring that everyone involved is following that same plan to help the student exert positive control over her environment.

Collect Data and Follow up to Analyze the Effectiveness of the Plan

Whenever the student engages in behaviors that are a part of the rage cycle, a *Crisis Report Form* should be completed (see Figure 2.5). This form documents student behaviors, interventions implemented at each stage, and their effectiveness. Educators and parents should meet according to a predetermined schedule to compare the student's baseline data to intervention data and information summarized on the *Crisis Report Form*. This analysis will help the team determine the effectiveness of the intervention. If successful, the plan may need to be continued with possible modifications and adaptations. If, on the other hand, the intervention is not as effective as hoped, it may be necessary to reexamine the function of the behavior and develop and implement a new behavioral intervention plan and *Student Crisis Plan Sheet.*

Motivation Assessment Scale

by V. Mark Durand and Daniel B. Crimmins

Name _____ Rater _____ Date _____

Behavior Description _____

Setting Description _____

ITEM	RESPONSE						
	NEVER	ALMOST NEVER	SELDOM	HALF THE TIME	USUALLY	ALMOST ALWAYS	ALWAYS
1. Would the behavior occur continuously, over and over, if this person was left alone for long periods of time? (For example, several hours.)	0	1	2	3	4	5	6
2. Does the behavior occur following a request to perform a difficult task?	0	1	2	3	4	5	6
3. Does the behavior seem to occur in response to your talking to other persons in the room?	0	1	2	3	4	5	6
4. Does the behavior ever occur to get a toy, food or activity that this person has been told that he or she can't have?	0	1	2	3	4	5	6
5. Would the behavior occur repeatedly, in the same way, for very long periods of time, if no one was around? (For example, rocking back and forth for over an hour.)	0	1	2	3	4	5	6
6. Does the behavior occur when any request is made of this person?	0	1	2	3	4	5	6
7. Does the behavior occur whenever you stop attending to this person?	0	1	2	3	4	5	6
8. Does the behavior occur when you take away a favorite toy, food, or activity?	0	1	2	3	4	5	6
9. Does it appear to you that this person enjoys performing the behavior? (It feels, tastes, looks, smells, and/or sounds pleasing.)	0	1	2	3	4	5	6
10. Does this person seem to do the behavior to upset or annoy you when you are trying to get him or her to do what you ask?	0	1	2	3	4	5	6

Figure 2.2. Functional assessment instruments: *Motivation Assessment Scale.*

ITEM	RESPONSE						
	NEVER	ALMOST NEVER	SELDOM	HALF THE TIME	USUALLY	ALMOST ALWAYS	ALWAYS
11. Does this person seem to do the behavior to upset or annoy you when you are not paying attention to him or her? (For example, if you are sitting in a separate room, interacting with another person.)	0	1	2	3	4	5	6
12. Does the behavior stop occurring shortly after you give this person the toy, food or activity he or she has requested?	0	1	2	3	4	5	6
13. When the behavior is occurring, does this person seem calm and unaware of anything else going on around him or her?	0	1	2	3	4	5	6
14. Does the behavior stop occurring shortly after (one to five minutes) you stop working or making demands of this person?	0	1	2	3	4	5	6
15. Does this person seem to do the behavior to get you to spend some time with him or her?	0	1	2	3	4	5	6
16. Does the behavior seem to occur when this person has been told that he or she can't do something he or she had wanted to do?	0	1	2	3	4	5	6

SCORING

	Sensory	Escape	Attention	Tangible
	1. _____	2. _____	3. _____	4. _____
	5. _____	6. _____	7. _____	8. _____
	9. _____	10. _____	11. _____	12. _____
	13. _____	14. _____	15. _____	16. _____
Total score =	_____	_____	_____	_____
Mean score =	_____	_____	_____	_____
Relative ranking =	_____	_____	_____	_____

Figure 2.2. **Continued**

Copyright 1992 by Monaco & Associates Incorporated. All rights reserved. Duplication is strictly prohibited by United States law and international agreements. Copies of the MAS and MAS Administration Guide are available by calling 785-272-5501. Used with permission.

Problem Behavior Questionnaire

RESPONDENT INFORMATION

Student _____ DOB _____ Grade _____ Sex M F   IEP: Y N

Teacher _____ School _____

Telephone _____ Date _____

STUDENT BEHAVIOR

Please briefly describe the problem behavior(s)

DIRECTIONS: Keeping in mind a typical episode of the problem behavior, circle the frequency at which each of the following statements is true.

	Never	10% of the time	25% of the time	50% of the time	75% of the time	90% of the time	All of the time
1. Does the problem behavior occur and persist when you make a request to perform a task?	0	1	2	3	4	5	6
2. When the problem behavior occurs do you redirect the student to get back to task or follow rules?	0	1	2	3	4	5	6
3. During a conflict with peers, if the student engages in the problem behavior do peers leave the student alone?	0	1	2	3	4	5	6
4. When the problem behavior occurs do peers verbally respond or laugh at the student?	0	1	2	3	4	5	6

Figure 2.2. Functional assessment instruments: Problem Behavior Questionnaire.

	Never	10% of the time	25% of the time	50% of the time	75% of the time	90% of the time	All of the time
5. Is the problem behavior more likely to occur following a conflict outside of the classroom? (e.g., bus write-up)	0	1	2	3	4	5	6
6. Does the problem behavior occur to get your attention when you are working with other students?	0	1	2	3	4	5	6
7. Does the problem behavior occur in the presence of specific peers?	0	1	2	3	4	5	6
8. Is the problem behavior more likely to continue to occur throughout the day following an earlier episode?	0	1	2	3	4	5	6
9. Does the problem behavior occur during specific academic activities?	0	1	2	3	4	5	6
10. Does the problem behavior stop when peers stop interacting with the student?	0	1	2	3	4	5	6
11. Does the behavior occur when peers are attending to other students?	0	1	2	3	4	5	6
12. If the student engages in the problem behavior do you provide 1-to-1 instruction to get student back on task?	0	1	2	3	4	5	6
13. Will the student stop doing the problem behavior if you stop making requests or end an academic activity?	0	1	2	3	4	5	6
14. If the student engages in the problem behavior, do peers stop interacting with the student?	0	1	2	3	4	5	6
15. Is the problem behavior more likely to occur following unscheduled events or disruptions in classroom routines?	0	1	2	3	4	5	6

Figure 2.2. Continued

Problem Behavior Questionnaire Profile

DIRECTIONS: Circle the score given for each question from the scale below the corresponding question number (in bold).

	PEERS						ADULTS						SETTING EVENTS		
	Escape			Attention			Escape			Attention					
	3	**10**	**14**	**4**	**7**	**11**	**1**	**9**	**13**	**2**	**6**	**12**	**5**	**8**	**15**
	6	6	6	6	6	6	6	6	6	6	6	6	6	6	6
	5	5	5	5	5	5	5	5	5	5	5	5	5	5	5
	4	4	4	4	4	4	4	4	4	4	4	4	4	4	4
	3	3	3	3	3	3	3	3	3	3	3	3	3	3	3
	2	2	2	2	2	2	2	2	2	2	2	2	2	2	2
	1	1	1	1	1	1	1	1	1	1	1	1	1	1	1
	0	0	0	0	0	0	0	0	0	0	0	0	0	0	0

Figure 2.2. Continued

Lewis, T. J., Scott, T. M., & Sugai, G. (1994). The problem behavior questionnaire: A teacher-based instrument to develop functional hypotheses of problem behavior in general education classrooms. *Diagnostique, 19*(2-3), 103-115. Reprinted with permission.

Student-Assisted
Functional-Assessment Interview

Student _____

Date _____

Interviewer _____

SECTION I

1. In general, is your work too hard for you?	ALWAYS	SOMETIMES	NEVER
2. In general, is your work too easy for you?	ALWAYS	SOMETIMES	NEVER
3. When you ask for help appropriately, do you get it?	ALWAYS	SOMETIMES	NEVER
4. Do you think work periods for each subject are too long?	ALWAYS	SOMETIMES	NEVER
5. Do you think work periods for each subject are too short?	ALWAYS	SOMETIMES	NEVER
6. When you do seatwork, do you do better when someone works with you?	ALWAYS	SOMETIMES	NEVER
7. Do you think people notice when you do a good job?	ALWAYS	SOMETIMES	NEVER
8. Do you think you get the points or rewards you deserve when you do good work?	ALWAYS	SOMETIMES	NEVER
9. Do you think you would do better in school if you received more rewards?	ALWAYS	SOMETIMES	NEVER
10. In general, do you find your work interesting?	ALWAYS	SOMETIMES	NEVER
11. Are there things in the classroom that distract you?	ALWAYS	SOMETIMES	NEVER
12. Is your work challenging enough for you?	ALWAYS	SOMETIMES	NEVER

SECTION II

1. When do you think you have the fewest problems with _____ in school?

   Why do you not have problems during this/these time(s)?

Figure 2.2. **Functional assessment instruments:**
Student-Assisted Functional-Assessment Interview.

2. When do you think you have the most problems with _____ in school?

   Why do you have problems during this/these time(s)?

3. What changes could be made so you would have fewer problems with _____ ?

4. What kinds of rewards would you like to earn for good behavior or good school work?

5. What are your favorite activities at school?

6. What are your hobbies or interests?

7. If you had the chance, what activities would you like to do that you don't have the opportunity to do?

SECTION III

Rate how much you like the following subjects:

	not at all		fair		very much
Reading	1	2	3	4	5
Math	1	2	3	4	5
Spelling	1	2	3	4	5
Handwriting	1	2	3	4	5
Science	1	2	3	4	5
English	1	2	3	4	5
Music	1	2	3	4	5
PE	1	2	3	4	5
Computers	1	2	3	4	5
Art	1	2	3	4	5

Figure 2.2. Continued

SECTION IV

What do you like about Reading?

What don't you like about Reading?

What do you like about Math?

What don't you like about Math?

What do you like about Spelling?

What don't you like about Spelling?

What do you like about Handwriting?

What don't you like about Handwriting?

What do you like about Science?

What don't you like about Science?

What do you like about Social Studies?

What don't you like about Social Studies?

What do you like about English?

What don't you like about English?

What do you like about Music?

What don't you like about Music?

What do you like about PE?

What don't you like about PE?

What do you like about Computers?

What don't you like about Computers?

What do you like about Art?

What don't you like about Art?

Figure 2.2. **Continued**

Kern, L., Dunlap, G., Clarke, S., & Childs, K. (1994). Student-assisted functional assessment interview. *Diagnostique, 19*(2-3), 29-39. Reprinted with permission.

Behavioral Intervention Plan

Student _____   School _____

Date Developed_____   Date Implemented_____

Grade_____

Baseline Data Results:

Hypothesis Statement:

Person(s) Responsible for Implementing Plan:

DESCRIPTION OF THE BEHAVIOR:

Behavior	Behavior Defined

INTERVENTION GOAL:

Figure 2.3. Sample behavioral intervention plan.

INTERVENTION PLAN:

1.

2.

3.

4.

5.

WHEN AND WHERE THE PLAN WILL BE IMPLEMENTED:

Figure 2.3. Continued

INTERVENTION DATA COLLECTION SUMMARY:

_____

_____

FOLLOW-UP AND REVIEW DATE(S):

COMMENTS:

TEAM MEETING PARTICIPANTS:

Name	Position
_____	_____
_____	_____
_____	_____
_____	_____
_____	_____

Figure 2.3. Continued

©McConnel, Hilvitz, & Cox, 1997. Developed for Turner Unified School District #202, Kansas City, KS. Reprinted with permission.

Student Crisis Plan Sheet

Student Name _____   Student Age/Grade _____

Teacher Name _____   Date of Plan _____

ENVIRONMENTAL/PERSONNEL CONSIDERATIONS

1. Describe how you can obtain assistance when it is needed _____
_____
_____

2. At which stage should outside assistance be sought?

_____ rumbling   _____ rage   _____ recovery

3. Which school personnel are available to provide assistance?

_____ principal   _____ school psychologist   _____ paraprofessional
_____ social worker   _____ counselor
_____ other (please specify) _____
_____ other (please specify) _____

4. Where should child(ren) exit to? (specify room or school) _____

5. At what stage should the plan be used by others in the classroom?

_____ rumbling   _____ rage   _____ recovery

6. Are there any extenuating circumstances that others should know about this
student (i.e., medications, related medical conditions, home situation)?

7. Who should be notified of the incident? _____

8. How should the incident be documented? _____

Figure 2.4. Student crisis plan sheet.

RUMBLING STAGE

---

1. What environmental factors/activities or antecedents lead to "rumbling" behaviors?

_____ unplanned change   _____ difficult assignment   _____ crowds
_____ teacher criticism   _____ transitions   _____ conflict with classmate
_____ other (please describe) _____

2. What behaviors does the student exhibit during the rumbling stage?

_____ bites nails   _____ tenses muscles   _____ stares
_____ taunts others   _____ refuses to work   _____ fidgets
_____ other (please describe) _____
_____ other (please describe) _____

3. Does the student mention any of the following complaints or illness?

_____ stomachache   _____ headache   _____ not applicable
_____ other (please describe) _____

4. Should the student be sent to the nurse if there is a complaint of illness?

_____ yes   _____ no

5. How long does the rumbling stage last before it progresses to the next stage?

_____

6. What interventions should be used at this stage?

_____ antiseptic bouncing   _____ proximity control   _____ touch control
_____ "just walk and don't talk" _____ home base   _____ redirecting
_____ other (please specify) _____
                              _____
_____ other (please specify) _____
                              _____

Figure 2.4. **Continued**

RAGE STAGE

1. What behaviors does the student exhibit during the rage stage?

_____ student verbally lashes   _____ student verbally lashes
out at teacher   out at students
_____ student threatens to hit teacher _____ student threatens to hit students
_____ student destroys materials   _____ student attempts to leave
                                       classroom
_____ student withdraws from teacher   _____ student hurts self
_____ other (please specify) _____
_____ other (please specify) _____

2. What teacher interventions should be used during this stage?

_____ physically move child to safe room   _____ prompt child to move to safe room
_____ remove others from the classroom   _____ redirect student
_____ other (please specify) _____
_____ other (please specify) _____

3. What is the role of others in the child's environment during the rage stage?_____
_____
_____

RECOVERY STAGE

1. What behaviors does the student exhibit during the recovery stage without intervention?

_____ sullenness   _____ withdrawal into fantasy   _____ denial
_____ "typical" student behavior
_____ other (please describe) _____
_____ other (please describe) _____

2. What supportive techniques should be used during this stage?_____
_____
_____

3. What interventions should be used at a later time to assist the student in gaining more self-control?_____
_____
_____

Figure 2.4. **Continued**

Crisis Report Form

Student Name _____

Teacher Name _____

Setting _____ Date _____

Antecedent Events _____

Rumbling Stage

Student Behavior _____

_____

Teacher Interventions _____

_____

Rage Stage

Student Behavior _____

_____

Teacher Interventions _____

_____

Recovery Stage

Student Behavior _____

_____

Teacher Interventions _____

_____

Other Considerations

_____

_____

_____

Figure 2.5. Crisis report form.

Classroom Measures for Preventing Behavioral Outbursts

Prevention, rather than intervention, is the most effective way to work with students who exhibit rage behaviors. Specifically, educators should invest time engaging in preventive actions in an effort to avoid the occurrence of many crises.

Train Others to Respond to Rage

Teachers and other staff must be trained to use various individualized intervention programs and know when to use various crisis procedures. Written operating procedures that clarify both general methods and procedures and programs for individual students can facilitate consistency, efficiency, and continuity. These procedures should delineate staff members' roles, interventions, crisis communication options, and evaluation methods. Training for participating staff should also include precise discussion of methods, modeling of various procedures, and role-playing.

Practice for a Crisis

In a manner similar to practicing for the eventuality of a fire, tornado or hurricane, students and staff should be prepared for a crisis involving rage. For example, students and staff should be aware of (a) where to go during times when students have rage attacks (i.e., what exits to use, where in the room to go, etc.); (b) who should be notified, how these contacts will occur, who will make the contacts, etc.; (c) what students not involved in crises should do during these occurrences; and (d) roles of various staff members during crises.

Dress for Possible Rage Attacks

Educators who are required to intervene with students are advised to dress in a fashion that will not interfere with their ability to appropriately respond to student outbursts. While specific dress and grooming choices are a function of a variety of factors, many educators have reported that wearing low-heeled shoes, choosing loose-fitting garments, eliminating sharp jewelry and dangling earrings, and choosing short hair styles or wearing hair pulled back increases their confidence and effectiveness.

Remove Items of Monetary and Sentimental Value from Reach of Students

It is common for out-of-control students to attempt to throw or destroy materials and items that are important to their teachers. Accordingly, such items should be removed from the classroom or kept out of reach of students who may lose control.

Establish Trust and Rapport with Students

Merely having a positive relationship with students will probably not eliminate their rage behaviors. Nonetheless, rapport does facilitate effective use of a variety of verbal interventions and other less intrusive crisis prevention and intervention methods. Hence, educators should consistently and clearly demonstrate positive attitudes and values toward students. Moreover, they should consistently model appropriate ways of dealing with frustration and anger, demonstrating to students that even though everyone (including teachers!) experiences stressful situations, there are alternatives to rage.

Delineate Expectations

A range of interventions commensurate with stages of rage and student individual histories and needs should be available. Clear identification of rules and other boundaries can help minimize rage attacks or meltdowns. Students should know what behaviors they can and cannot engage in within the classroom setting. It is not enough that students are told expectations, they must be taught expectations to ensure understanding.

Provide Consistent Consequences for Rule Compliance and Noncompliance

Students respond best to clearly structured settings wherein consistent positive and negative consequences exist for their behavior. While there are exceptions to this rule (e.g., a student's profanities might be ignored during rage; a student's obscene gesture may "not be seen" by her teacher following a crisis involving property violence, permitting the student to "save face"), students generally respond best to clearly identified and enforced standards.

Remain Calm and in Control During Rage Attacks

Accomplishing such control is primarily a function of training, practice and experience. During a crisis, teachers should calmly communicate to students that staff are there to assist them. It is recommended that teachers not threaten students. Rather, students should be calmly instructed in rules and consequences, and what they need to do to end a crisis (e.g., "as soon as you are quietly seated, we can discuss this"). Educators should also communicate to students that they are permitted to be upset and angry, albeit in socially acceptable ways. Further, it is recommended that teachers and staff who engage students on the verge of or demonstrating rage focus on the "what" of the behavior, rather than the "why." Finally, teachers should not argue with students or provide ammunition for arguments. Educators must be willing to admit that they will not win arguments with students and hence work actively not to engage in these interactions. It is much more productive to acknowledge students' feelings ("It's ok to be angry–sit down and we can talk about it"), ignore accusations, and assertively focus on steps needed to resolve crises of rage.

Maintain a Therapeutic Attitude

Students with Asperger Syndrome tend to be most responsive to educators who demonstrate attitudes and behaviors that communicate support, respect, and a willingness to assist. Thus, educators are strongly advised to seek avenues for maintaining students' dignity and esteem. One component of a therapeutic attitude includes a willingness to understand students and consider their emotional fragility. Empathy for students assists educators in seeking appropriate ways of dealing with problem behavior and implementing intervention programs.

Educators should intervene in a timely manner with students who are prone to experience rage attacks. That is, communicating to a student that a teacher is concerned because the student is agitated, giving students options for gaining control, seeking alternatives to standard management procedures (e.g., suggesting to a student that he get a drink of water as a calming strategy), and intervening prior to a rule infraction, frequently have positive effects.

A therapeutic attitude also involves use of nonpunitive, supportive intervention programs. For example, educators should never require a student to apologize before being released from a restraint hold, belittle a student, or humiliate a child for her inappropriate behavior. Educators should be willing to ignore student remarks and gestures that occur during crises when these behaviors are attempts to salvage dignity, maintain control, or preserve ego.

Finally, educators involved with students with Asperger Syndrome who exhibit rage attacks or meltdowns should be reminded that in spite of the emotions evoked by these students, and in spite of the difficulties they may cause, educators are commissioned to assist these young people in acquiring skills and knowledge that will assist them in the future.

Systemwide Policies and Procedures Needed to Meet the Needs of Aggressive and Violent Students

Effectively serving children and youth with Asperger Syndrome who experience rage in various school settings requires consideration of procedures beyond the students' immediate classrooms and teachers. Thus, several policies must be in place aimed at creating systems that are supportive or responsive to the needs of these individuals.

Offer a Full Continuum of Services

Many students with Asperger Syndrome who have rage attacks can succeed in general education classrooms. However, it is best for these students to be assigned to settings based on their individual needs. Educators should have available a range of options for these students, including social service, mental health, vocational, and legal services. It is important that the environment be "user friendly" and that school personnel enforce school rules without obstructing typical student activities any more than absolutely necessary. A variety of instructional approaches and materials should be available to assist students experiencing academic and social difficulties. Support programs should also be available to students, including peer tutoring and cooperative learning arrangements.

Enhance Communication Across Agencies and Disciplines

To ensure that student and family needs are met in an efficient and timely manner, and to orchestrate services, efficient and effective communication lines must be established between and among schools and agencies. Such a communication system ensures information sharing, thereby preventing individuals within various systems from losing contact with one another, from failing to make appropriate service provisions, or from duplicating services.

A liaison should be established between schools, institutional settings, social services and other community-based agencies. The role of liaison or case manager should be assumed by professionals capable of developing and maintaining rapport and effectively communicating with staff in their respective schools and agencies, as well as with parents and families. The case manager serves as coordinator of services for students from their particular school or agency, ensuring that they are provided in a timely and appropriate manner.

Facilitate Parent and Family Involvement and Provide Maximum Family Support

Parents and families play an important role in supporting children and youth with problems of rage. In fact, parent and family support systems are often the bridge to long-term solutions to problems of rage. Relative to assisting school and agency personnel, parents and families may provide important information on student needs and characteristics; they can provide an important link between school and community; and they can be directly involved in developing and implementing intervention programs. Implicit in such involvement is professionals' willingness to empower parents and families to be actively involved in intervention and communication programs based on their needs, interests and abilities. Parent and family empowerment requires professional willingness and ability to train interested family members to be collaborators and team members.

Train and Empower a Liaison to Coordinate Programs and Services

A school-based liaison or case manager should be assigned to each student. Responsibilities of case managers include (a) coordinating student services and programs across agencies and schools; (b) acting as the primary liaison between educators, agency personnel and parents; (c) organizing student records and information; (d) synthesizing student information for appropriate personnel; and (e) coordinating student education and intervention programs. Case managers may also train others to serve students with Asperger Syndrome who are prone to rage attacks.

Summary

Students with Asperger Syndrome who exhibit rage attacks are most often served in general education settings. Thus, it is important that school-based personnel are able to plan and apply appropriate interventions for these students. In this regard, it is imperative that teachers understand the rage cycle and how to intervene at each stage. It is also crucial that school-based personnel work together to devise and implement policies to meet the needs of these students. It is through these strategies that students with a propensity for rage will have an opportunity to succeed in a public school setting.

CHAPTER

Strategies That Promote Self-Awareness, Self-Calming, and Self-Management

Children and youth with Asperger Syndrome do not want to engage in rage behaviors. Rather, for most of these children and youth, the rage cycle is the only way they know of expressing stress, problems with coping, or a host of other emotions to which they see no solution. Most want to learn methods to facilitate self-awareness of their emotions and techniques to manage their behavior and calm themselves in the face of problems. In fact, if children not in the midst of the rage cycle are approached by someone with whom they have rapport, and are introduced to strategies that are compatible with their learning style and the behavior functions or triggers that are causing problems, they are generally willing learners. *The best intervention to rage is prevention.* Prevention occurs best as a multi-faceted approach consisting of (a) instruction, (b) interpretation, and (c) restructuring.

Instruction includes providing direct assistance to children and youth with Asperger Syndrome in skill provision, such as using a scope and sequence chart to identify skill areas in which the child may be deficient and providing direct instruction to teach those skills. *Interpretation* is the recognition that, no matter how well developed the skills of the person with Asperger Syndrome, situations will arise that he or she does not understand. As a result, someone in the person's environment must serve as an interpreter using a variety of techniques, including cartooning or social autopsies. The third element in this multifaceted approach, *restructuring*, is the recognition that the person with Asperger Syndrome has an exceptionality for which accommodations must be made. Ideally, the individual will learn to restructure her own environment or request environmental modifications that aid in social understanding. This chapter discusses several interventions that fit within this approach. Many of the interventions overviewed here fit into more than one of the three categories. For example, social stories (Gray & Gerand, 1993) can serve as both an instructional and an interpretive tool.

Instruction

Students with Asperger Syndrome demonstrate many social and behavioral deficits and differences that require instruction to ensure acquisition of skills that facilitate self-awareness, self-calming, and self-management. Most often, these students do not acquire many of the skills that we take for granted without a planned instructional sequence. Some considerations for instruction include (a) scope and sequence, (b) direct instruction, (c) social stories, (d) hidden curriculum, (e) acting lessons, and (f) self-esteem building.

Scope and Sequence

Because children and youth with Asperger Syndrome evidence an uneven profile of social, behavioral, and communication skills, it is important to understand the sequence in which these skills develop. Without an understanding of scope and sequence, it is possible to overlook that a child may be missing an important prerequisite skill that might make a more advanced skill become rote-based instead of a usable asset. For example, if a student does not understand that tone of voice communicates a message, then teaching the more advanced skill of using a respectful tone of voice to teachers may have little or no meaning. If the student learns by rote to use that tone of voice, it most likely will not be generalized.

Several scope and sequences exist that outline skills that specifically support self-awareness, self-calming, and self-management. Howlin, Baron-Cohen, and Hadwin (1999) provide a sequence of developmental and instructional strategies for the five levels of emotional understanding, the five levels of informational state understanding, and the five levels of pretend play (see Table 3.1).

Table 3.1
An Overview of Skill Sequence and Instructional Strategies from "Teaching Children with Autism to Mind-Read: A Practical Guide" by Howlin, Baron-Cohen, & Hadwin (1999)

The Five Levels of Emotional Understanding

Level 1: Recognizing facial expression from photographs

Level 2: Recognizing emotion from schematic drawings

Level 3: Identifying "situation-based" emotions

Level 4: Identifying "desire-based" emotions

Level 5: Identifying "belief-based" emotions

The Five Levels of Informational State Understanding

Level 1: Simple visual perspective taking

Level 2: Complex visual perspective taking

Level 3: Understanding the principle that "seeing leads to knowing"

Level 4: Predicting actions on the basis of a person's knowledge

Level 5: Understanding false beliefs

The Five Levels of Pretend Play

Level 1: Sensorimotor play

Level 2: Emerging functional play

Level 3: Established functional play

Level 4: Emerging pretend play

Level 5: Established pretend play

From: Howlin, P., Baron-Cohen, S., & Hadwin, J. (1999). *Teaching children with autism to mind-read: A practical guide.* London: John Wiley & Sons (pp. v, vi). Used with permission.

Howlin et al. also provide structured assessment in each of the areas, which includes establishing a baseline and teaching procedures that contain a strong visual component. For example, under teaching emotions, the authors provide instruction on identifying "situation-based" emotions. Figure 3.1 shows a sample of general teaching principles related to identifying "situation-based" emotions and one of the many visual scenarios used to teach this concept.

Duke, Nowicki, and Martin (1996) offer a school-based curriculum to teach nonverbal language in the areas of (a) paralanguage, (b) facial expression, (c) space and touch, (d) gestures and postures, (e) rhythm and time, (f) objectics, and (g) cross-channeling. For example, the facial expression unit contains lessons on (a) the resting face, (b) using eye contact, (c) horizontal zoning, (d) mimicking, (e) making faces, (f) varying the intensity of expression, (g) varying the angle of expression, and (h) object imaging. Nowicki and colleagues outline the features of a teaching and remediation program that are integrated into each of the nonverbal language areas as well as suggestions for how to facilitate the instructional process (see Table 3.2).

General Teaching Principle

Whether correct or incorrect, the child is always provided with the general principle underlying that emotion.

When someone gives you something nice/you do something exciting (etc.), then you feel happy.

When something scary happens, you feel frightened and want to run away/hide.

When something nasty happens accidentally/people leave (etc.), then you feel sad.

When someone does something nasty to you on purpose (etc.), then you feel angry.

Figure 3.1. A sample of general teaching principles related to identifying "situation-based" emotions and a visual scenario used to teach this concept.

Frightening Situations

Teacher: Describe the picture to the child and ask the child either to say how the person in the story feels, or to point to one of the emotion faces below.

The big dog is chasing Dan down the road.

Emotion Question: How will Dan feel when the dog chases him?
Prompt–will he feel happy/sad/angry/afraid?

Justification Question: Why will he feel happy/sad/angry/afraid?

Figure 3.1. Continued

From: Howlin, P., Baron-Cohen, S., & Hadwin, J. (1999). *Teaching children with autism to mind-read: A practical guide.* New York: John Wiley and Sons, Inc. Used with permission.

Table 3.2
Features of the Teaching and Remediation Program of "Teaching Your Child the Language of Social Success" by Duke, Nowicki, & Martin (1996)

The purpose of teaching and remediation is to develop or improve skills. All of the activities in this book [*Teaching Your Child the Language of Social Success*] are designed to be:

- **systematic**: to teach in an organized way that makes sense to the pupil

- **ordered or graded**: to disclose increasingly complex information

- **cumulative**: to build and thoroughly explore each learning process before progressing to the next

- **multisensory**: to integrate visual, auditory, and tactile modalities

- **sympathetic**: to instill the confidence in each individual that a tutor understands his or her specific difficulties and wants to help

The following suggestions will facilitate the teaching and remediation process for all students, no matter their level of nonverbal communication skill:

- Maintain the child's interest.

- Set goals. Work on one area of improvement at a time.

- Give individual attention as frequently as possible. Encourage the student to ask many questions.

- Deliver new material more than once. Review and reinforcement are necessary.

- Help the student to relate new skills to past experience.

- Be positive and work on building the student's self-esteem.

- Allow children to learn any way they can, using any tools available.

- Practice.

- Practice.

- Practice!

From: Duke, M.P., Nowicki, S., & Martin, E.A. (1996). *Teaching your child the language of social success.* Atlanta, GA: Peachtree (pp. 32-33). Used with permission.

Direct Instruction

Children with Asperger Syndrome do not innately develop the social and behavioral skills necessary to be successful in school, home, and the community. As a result, teachers must provide an effective instructional sequence that facilitates student skill acquisition, including (a) rationale, (b) presentation, (c) modeling, (d) verification, (e) evaluation, and (f) generalization.

Rationale

Students with Asperger Syndrome often need to understand how or why concepts required for mastery are relevant. Thus, teachers must relate to the student (a) why the information is useful, (b) how the student can use the information, and (c) where it fits in with the knowledge the student already possesses. The rationale should also include a visual task analysis that illustrates all the components of the lesson, including the amount of time to be spent on the lesson and activities to follow. Similar to students with other exceptionalities, students with Asperger Syndrome need to understand lesson rationale before they can or will learn.

Presentation

The teacher tells and shows the student the goals for the presented content and spells out exactly what the student needs to learn. Then, through a direct instructional format, the content is taught using visual and auditory stimuli. Information is broken down into small increments and presented. This type of instruction is active, with the teacher presenting information, asking questions, and providing corrective feedback. In other words, direct instruction does not mean presenting a worksheet with a model and telling the student to follow the directions.

Modeling

During the model phase, the teacher obtains the student's attention and shows him what he is supposed to do. The instructor demonstrates how to participate in a cooperative group activity or how to use a specific paralanguage strategy. It is also important to demonstrate how to complete the task or assignment correctly, instead of telling the student what not to do. Many students with Asperger Syndrome may know what not to do, but have no understanding of what is required of them.

Models should be presented frequently. Every direction is explicitly spelled out for the student, preferably with a visual component. The teacher cannot infer that the student understands a specific concept or format just because it has been presented before. Anything that is merely implied by the teacher will likely *not* be understood by the student.

Verification

Throughout the lesson, the teacher must closely monitor the student's emotional state. Because students with Asperger Syndrome often have a flat, even seemingly negative affect, it is difficult to tell when they are stressed as a result of not comprehending specific content. The teacher must work with the student to understand how she communicates emotional distress and meet that student's needs as necessary, through additional instruction, modeling, or individual work sessions. Failure to engage in this very important step can result in the student "tuning out" or having a rage attack.

Because of a propensity for tunnel vision and distraction/inattention, the student with Asperger Syndrome must be actively engaged throughout the instructional process. For example, the student should be provided physical cues to attend to relevant stimuli and be asked frequent questions. Physical cues could come in the form of the teacher using proximity control and tapping briefly on the student's desk using a prearranged signal (clearing the throat; placing a pencil on the student's desk; placing a hand on the student's shoulder).

For the student with Asperger Syndrome who requires a long processing time, the teacher might want to use a prearranged strategy so that the student knows when she will be asked a question. For example, the teacher might tell the student that she will only be asked a question when the teacher stands next to her. The teacher then uses this strategy, initially asking questions to which the student knows the answers. As the student becomes comfortable with the strategy and grows more confident, the teacher can introduce questions that might be more difficult. No one else in the class needs to be aware that the student and teacher have this agreement.

Evaluation

Following instruction, skill acquisition requires evaluation from both the teacher and the student. The teacher should employ a variety of methods to assess student understanding and use of the skill. Students should also participate in the process, self-evaluating their skill performance and setting goals for generalization and skill maintenance.

Generalization

Programming for generalization should be a part of every lesson through opportunities for students to use newly acquired skills throughout the school day and in a variety of different settings (e.g., physical education class, music). Educators should also observe the student in less structured settings, such as lunch and recess, to determine whether the skill has truly been generalized. Assistance from parents is also invaluable to ensure generalization. Specifically, parents can set up and/or observe home- and community-based events in which the skill should be used.

Social Stories

Social stories are an effective method of providing both guidance and directions for responding to various social situations that promote self-awareness, self-calming, and self-management (Gray, 1994; Gray & Gerand, 1993; Swaggart et al., 1995). A *social story* describes social situations specific to individuals and circumstances. For instance, Josh, a third-grade student with Asperger Syndrome, often became agitated in the lunchroom when he perceived that his general education peers were too close to his "tray space." The child did not want other students to touch or be within several inches of his cafeteria tray. When his space was invaded, Josh would lash out against the perceived trespasser.

A social story was developed to deal with this problem. It described Josh, the setting, the peers and adults in the lunchroom, and the child's feelings and perceptions of the setting: Josh liked to eat near his peers but did not want his tray touched. The social story also described appropriate responses for Josh in the setting, including (a) sitting at the end of the assigned lunch table, (b) taking his food from the tray and placing it on the table, and (c) placing the tray under his seat. Josh was then to eat his lunch, take his tray and remaining items to the designated disposal area, and return to visit with his friends until lunch was over. The social story also discussed Josh's feelings if his space was still encroached upon and gave him some statements that he could appropriately use if he felt crowded. Finally, the story included some brief statements concerning the perspective of others who were crowding Josh. This social story and others like it involve structuring individual behavior and social responses by offering individualized and specific response cues. Table 3.3 provides one example of guidelines that can be used to structure a social story for an individual with Asperger Syndrome.

Hidden Curriculum

Every school, and indeed every society, has a hidden curriculum–the dos and don'ts that are not spelled out but that everyone somehow knows about (Bieber, 1994). For example, everyone knows that Mrs. Kristmann allows students to whisper in class as long as they get their work done, whereas Mrs. Rafik does not tolerate any level of noise in her class. Everyone knows that Mr. Johnson, the assistant principal, is a stickler for following the rules, so no one curses or even slouches in his presence. Everyone also knows that the really tough guys (the ones who like to beat up unsuspecting kids) hang out behind the slide, just out of teacher view. Everyone knows these things, that is, everyone except the student with Asperger Syndrome.

Outside of school, the hidden curriculum is an even bigger issue. For example, what is the hidden curriculum for attending a nice restaurant?

1. You call ahead for reservations.
2. Upon arrival, you wait to be seated.
3. A waiter delivers a menu to you and may place a napkin in your lap.
4. And so on.

Somehow, a young person learns this hidden agenda. Perhaps he has been taught this curriculum by his grandmother; maybe he learned it from reading a book on etiquette. What if the student thinks the above is appropriate restaurant behavior anywhere and attempts to generalize it to McDonald's? How long will he wait to be seated?

Consider the hidden curriculum associated with a library visit. When a teenage girl goes to the library with her father, she is there to check out a book. She talks quietly to her father, selects a book, checks it out and leaves. This is one hidden curriculum for the library. However, there are other hidden curricula for the library. When a teenage girl goes to the library with her friends, for example, the curriculum is different. Chances are that she is not there to check out a book and that she will not talk quietly, unless she is prompted to do so. The hidden curriculum of going to the library with friends is to socialize, have fun, and not be kicked out of the library.

Students with Asperger Syndrome are at a disadvantage because they usually do not understand the hidden curriculum. They inadvertently break the

Table 3.3
Guidelines for Social Story Construction

1. Identify target behavior or problem situation.

A social behavior should be selected for change, preferably one whose improvement can result in (a) increased positive social interactions, (b) a safer environment, and/or (c) additional social learning opportunities. The behavior should be task-analyzed and based on the student's ability level.

2. Define target behavior.

The individuals who plan and implement social stories must clearly define the behavior on which data will be collected to ensure that everyone involved in the instructional process can reliably measure change. In addition, the behavior should be described in a way that facilitates student understanding.

3. Collect baseline data.

Baseline data should be collected over a period of at least three to five days. This will allow the educator and others to determine the trend of the behavior.

4. Write a short social story using descriptive, directive, perspective, and control sentences.

A good rule of thumb to follow in writing social stories is to use descriptive, perspective, and control sentences for every directive sentence in the story (Gray, 1994). Stories should be written in accordance with the student's comprehension skills, with vocabulary and print size individualized for each student. The stories should be written in the first person and either in the present (to describe a situation as it occurs) or the future tense (to anticipate an upcoming event).

5. Display story commensurate with student's functioning level.

For some students, one to three sentences per page is often adequate. Each sentence allows the student to focus on and process a specific concept. Depending on the student's skill level, more than one sentence per page may result in an overload of information such that the student is not able to comprehend the information presented.

Although Gray (1994) cautioned that illustrations may too narrowly define a situation, resulting in limited generalization, others (i.e., Kuttler, Myles, & Carlson, 1998; Swaggart et al., 1995) have found that pictorial representations can enhance student understanding of appropriate behavior, especially with students who lack reading skills. However, decisions about whether to use a pictorial representation with social stories should be made on an individual basis.

Table 3.3 Continued

6. Read the social story to the student.

The teacher or student should read the social story as a consistent part of the student's daily schedule. Further, the student who is able to read independently may read the social story to peers so that all have a similar perspective of the targeted situation and appropriate behaviors.

7. Collect intervention data.

Data should be collected throughout the social story intervention process, using the procedures that were used to gather baseline data.

8. Review findings.

If desired behavioral changes fail to occur after implementing the social story intervention for two weeks, review the social story and its implementation procedures. If program alterations are made, it is recommended that only one variable be changed at a time (e.g., the content of the story, rather than simultaneously also changing the time the social story is read and the person who reads it). By changing one factor at a time, the instructor can determine the factor or factors that best facilitate individual learning.

9. Program for maintenance and generalization.

After a behavior change has been established consistently, the educator may want to fade use of the social story. Fading may be accomplished by extending the time between readings or by placing additional responsibility on students for reading their social story themselves. Finally, students with sufficient independent skills may be assisted in identifying social goals for which they may develop their own related social stories.

---

rules associated with the hidden curriculum and either get in trouble with adults or become further ostracized or hurt by peers. As a result, they require direct instruction on the hidden curriculum. They need to be taught that some middle school students curse, but no one curses in front of an adult, unless that adult is Ms. Gagnon who tends to ignore such things. They need to know that only nerds wear tight-legged, high-water jeans to school. They need to know never to argue with a policeman. Persons with Asperger Syndrome also need to know (a) teacher expectations, (b) teacher-pleasing behaviors, (c) students to interact with and those to stay away from, and (d) behaviors that attract positive and negative attention. Understanding the hidden curriculum can make all of the difference to students with Asperger Syndrome–it can keep them out of detention or worse, and it can help them make friends. Temple Grandin developed her own set of rules, many of which are from the hidden curriculum, to guide her social interactions and behavior in society (see Table 3.4).

Who should teach the hidden curriculum? Many teachers voice concern over teaching certain elements of the culture ("I can't tell them it is all right to curse in front of Ms. Gagnon."). There are many hidden curriculum elements that teachers can comfortably teach and should teach as they would reading, writing, or social studies. There are other elements on which teachers should not provide instruction. In these areas, peer models can be enlisted. However, this should be done carefully. It is recommended that peers identify hidden curriculum items and then meet to discuss them with teachers and the student's parents. As a group they can decide when, how, and if to provide instruction on these very important elements.

Acting Lessons

Many adults with Asperger Syndrome and higher-functioning autism suggest that acting lessons are an appropriate means of teaching children and youth about social and emotional issues to aid in self-awareness, self-calming, and self-management. During acting lessons, children learn to express verbally and nonverbally their emotions in specific situations. They also learn to interpret others' emotions, feelings, and voices. Perhaps more importantly, acting class participants engage in simulations and receive feedback from an instructor and peers regarding their performance. One adult with Asperger Syndrome, Margo, credits her success in expressing emotions and interpreting social situations to acting lessons. She acknowledges that her "real life" performances may be a bit stilted, but after acting classes she does understand better how to act and react in a neuro-typical world.

Self-Esteem Building

The child or youth with Asperger Syndrome may look different, act different, feel different, and, in some ways, *is* different from other people. The child often knows this. A loss of self-esteem is often the by-product. As adults, there is a high price to pay for a negative self-esteem. It has been documented that adults with Asperger Syndrome have higher levels of depression, suicide and other affective disorders than the general population, which can partially be related to self-concept problems (Baron-Cohen, 1988;

Table 3.4
Temple Grandin's Rule System to Guide Her Social Interactions and Behavior

Temple Grandin developed this rule system to guide her social interactions and behavior

1. Really Bad Things–examples: murder, arson, stealing, lying in court under oath, injuring or hitting other people. All cultures have prohibitions against really bad things because an orderly, civilized society cannot function if people are robbing and killing each other.

2. Courtesy Rules–do not cut in on a line at the movie theater or airport, observe table manners, say thank you, and keep yourself clean. These things are important because they make the other people around you more comfortable. I don't like it when somebody else has sloppy table manners, so I try to have decent table manners. It annoys me if somebody cuts in front of me in a line, so I do not do this to other people.

3. Illegal But Not Bad–examples: slight speeding on the freeway and illegal parking. However, parking in a handicapped zone would be worse because it would violate the courtesy rules.

4. Sins of the System (SOS)–examples: smoking pot (and being thrown in jail for ten years) and sexual misbehavior. SOS's are things where the penalty is so severe that it defies all logic. Sometimes, the penalty for sexual misbehavior is worse than killing somebody. Rules governing sexual behavior are so emotionally based that I do not dare discuss the subject for fear of committing an SOS. An SOS in one society may be acceptable behavior in another, whereas rules 1, 2, 3 tend to be more uniform between different cultures.

I have never done a sin of the system ... People with autism have to learn that certain behaviors will not be tolerated–period. You will be fired no matter how good your work is if you commit an SOS at work. People with autism and Asperger's need to learn that if they want to keep a job, they must not commit an SOS ... The social knowledge required is just too complex.

From: Grandin, T. (1999, April). *Understanding people with autism: Developing a career makes life satisfying.* Paper presented at the MAAP Services, Incorporated, and Indiana Resource Center for Autism Conference, Indianapolis, IN. Used with permission of MAAP Services, Inc., PO Box 524, Crown Point, IN, 46307, 219-662-1311, fax 219-662-0638 (chart@netnitco.net).

Berthier, Santamaria, Encabo, & Tolosa, 1992; Simblett & Wilson, 1993; Williams, 1995; Wing, 1981).

Educators and parents need to work together to help the child understand that she is more than the exceptionality. She is not Asperger Syndrome. She is a child who has this exceptionality–but this is only one part of her. She has many other characteristics, which need to be pointed out and celebrated (Bieber, 1994). In fact, aspects other than the disorder should be the primary focus of a conversation about Asperger Syndrome. The child with this exceptionality should understand that all people are special. Everyone has things they do well and things that are challenging. It is possible for the exceptionality to receive so much attention and focus that it becomes the major facet of the child's identity.

The child needs assistance in developing a positive self-image. This is built, in part, by successful experiences. LaVoie (cited in Bieber, 1994) poignantly challenges teachers and parents to find the "island of competence" in the child, stress it and celebrate it. Presenting multiple opportunities for the child to demonstrate his "island of competence" builds self-esteem.

Strategies to build self-esteem include:

1. Place the child with Asperger Syndrome in the role as a helper or tutor.
2. Tell the child what he is doing right. Reframe negative language to positive language.
3. Find what the child does well and help her do more of it.
4. Compliment the child and teach him to compliment himself.

Interpretation

Social situations occur daily or even hourly that make little or no sense to the person with Asperger Syndrome but are taken for granted by the general population. These individuals often end up in trouble because they could not understand a direction or intent. Even when the person with Asperger Syndrome receives effective instruction in the social and behavioral realms, situations will occur that require interpretation. A number of interpretative strategies can help turn seemingly random actions into meaningful interactions for individuals with Asperger Syndrome. These include: (a) sensory awareness, such as that offered by the Alert Program; (b) cartooning; (c) social autopsies; (d) the Situation, Options, Consequences, Choices, Strategies, Simulation (SOCCSS) strategy; and (e) video detective.

Sensory Awareness

All of the information children receive from their environment comes through the sensory system. Taste, smell, sight, sound, touch, movement, the force of gravity and body position are the basic sensory ingredients that enable all children and youth to listen, attend for a period of time, and to be calm enough or awake enough to participate in learning experiences (Anderson & Emmons, 1996; Ayres, 1979; Williams & Shellenberger, 1996). Teachers and parents of children and youth with Asperger Syndrome often assume, erroneously, that these children have an intact sensory system. This is not the case; many of these children have sensory integration dysfunction (Orr et al., 1999). That is, they have neurological differences that do not allow them to process information or respond appropriately or in a timely manner.

Recognizing the sensory differences that exist within individuals and acknowledging that children and youth, such as those with Asperger Syndrome, can learn to self-regulate their sensory systems, Williams and Shellenberger (1996) developed a sensory integration program entitled, *How Does Your Engine Run: A Leader's Guide to the Alert Program for Self-Regulation.* Designed for use by occupational therapists in conjunction with other educators and parents, this ingenious program helps children to recognize their sensory needs. In addition, children and youth learn to recognize their level of alertness or arousal and change that level as necessary to meet academic or social demands.

The Alert Program "uses the analogy of an automobile engine to introduce its concepts of self-regulation to students. 'If your body is like a car engine, sometimes it runs on high, sometimes it runs on low, and sometimes it runs just right'" (Williams & Shellenberger, 1996, pp. 2-1). Williams and Shellenberger provide instruction in 3 stages and 12 mile markers (see Table 3.5).

For example, through the Alert Program Susan has learned to recognize that her level of alertness is high as she enters school—she feels anxious and jittery. She also realizes that she needs a lower level of alertness to pay attention during her first class—math. From the curriculum, she knows how to change her level of alertness. She knows that if she sits quietly for about 10 minutes and listens to some quiet music with headphones, she will be ready to attend to math instruction. Susan moves to provide herself with the activities that will change her level of alertness.

Table 3.5
3 Stages and 12 Mile Markers
of the Alert Program

STAGE ONE: Identifying Engine Speeds

1. Students learn the engine words.
2. Adults label their own engine levels.
3. Students develop awareness of the feel of their own engine speeds, using the adults' labels as their guides.
4. Students learn to identify and label levels for themselves.
5. Students label levels for themselves, outside therapy sessions.

STAGE TWO: Experimenting with Methods to Change Engine Speeds

6. Leaders introduce sensorimotor methods to change engine levels.
7. Leaders identify sensorimotor preferences and sensory hypersensitivities.
8. Students begin experimentation with choosing strategies.

STAGE THREE: Regulating Engine Speeds

9. Students choose strategies independently.
10. Student use strategies independently, outside therapy sessions.
11. Students learn to change engine levels when options are limited.
12. Students continue receiving support.

From: Williams, M.S., & Shellenberger, S. (1996). *How does your engine run? A leader's guide to the alert program for self-regulation.* Used with permission of TherapyWorks, Inc., 4901 Butte Place N.W., Albuquerque, NM 87120, 505-897-3478, fax 505-899-4071 (www.AlertProgram.com).

Cartooning

Visual symbols, such as schedules and cartooning, have been found to enhance the processing abilities of persons with Asperger Syndrome and others in the autism spectrum and to enhance their understanding of the environment. Indeed, research has shown that visual support can serve as an effective means of teaching educational skills, functional living skills, and social skills (Kozleski, 1991; Krantz, MacDuff, & McClannahan, 1993; Kuttler et al., 1998). One type of visual support is cartooning. The technique, used as a generic term, has been implemented by speech/language pathologists for many years to enhance understanding in their clients. Speech/language pathologists have used this technique to illustrate the actual meaning of idioms as well as to interpret social situations. Used in a more specific way, cartooning plays an integral role in a number of intervention techniques: pragmaticism (Arwood, 1991), mind-reading (Hadwin, Baron-Cohen, Howlin, & Hill, 1996; Howlin et al., 1999) and comic strip conversations (Gray, 1994, 1995).

Comic strip conversations were introduced by Gray (1994, 1995) to illustrate and interpret social situations and provide support to "students who struggle to comprehend the quick exchange of information which occurs in a conversation" (p. 2). Comic strip conversations promote social understanding by incorporating simple figures and other symbols in a comic strip format. Speech, thought bubble symbols, and color are used to help the individual with Asperger Syndrome see and analyze a conversation. According to Attwood (1998), comic strip conversations "allow the child to analyze and understand the range of messages and meanings that are a natural part of conversation and play. Many children with Asperger's Syndrome are confused and upset by teasing or sarcasm. The speech and thought bubble as well as choice of colors can illustrate the hidden messages" (p. 72). An educator can draw a social situation in order to facilitate understanding or assist the student in doing her own illustrations.

The effectiveness of comic strip stories is only anecdotally reported. The following overviews a situation in which this technique was effective. Tom, a 14-year-old with Asperger Syndrome, was confused by conversations that girls were having with him. One in particular caused a rage attack. After Tom had regained self-control, his teacher asked him to relate the conversation that had distressed him while she cartooned what he said. Figure 3.2 shows Tom's conversation with a classmate, Mary, who had told him that he had a "cute butt." Tom, whose somewhat obsessive interest was legal issues, thought he was being sexually harassed by Mary and called her a "sexist pig." Mary retorted by calling him a jerk. In kind, Tom repeated the comment. Tom's teacher helped him to understand, through the use of a comic strip conversation, that Mary was most likely trying to say that she liked Tom and that her feelings were hurt when she did not receive the expected response (an acknowledgment of her affection). The situation may have been further compounded when Mary was called a pig, particularly as she perceived herself as having a weight problem and might have interpreted this remark as being directed toward that issue. Following the session with his teacher, Tom was able to understand Mary's hidden message and that he had probably hurt her feelings. He then made plans to apologize to Mary for having misunderstood her (Rogers & Myles, 1999).

Tom at this point said the author, "I don't think she's fat but I should not call her a pig. I need to tell her I'm sorry."

Figure 3.2. Sample comic strip conversation.

Social Autopsies

Social autopsies are particularly well suited to interpret social and behavioral situations Developed by LaVoie (cited in Bieber, 1994) to help students with severe learning and social problems understand social mistakes, a social skills autopsy is used to dissect social incidents so that individuals learn from their mistakes. When a social mistake occurs, the individual with Asperger Syndrome meets with a teacher, counselor, or parent. Together, in a non-punitive fashion, they identify the mistake and determine who was harmed by it. Then the student develops a plan to ensure that the error does not reoccur. Because of the visual strengths, problem-solving deficits, and language processing problems of students with Asperger Syndrome, social skills autopsies may be enhanced by using written words or phrases or pictorial representations to illustrate each of the stages. LaVoie overviewed the attributes and nonattributes of social autopsies, reiterating that it is a supportive, interpretive technique (see Table 3.6).

Table 3.6
Attributes and Nonattributes of Social Autopsies

A social autopsy is ...	A social autopsy is not ...
• Supportive, structured, constructive	• Punishment
• Solution-oriented	• Negative
• Opportunity for student participation	• Controlled and conducted by an adult
• A process for interpretation	• A "one-time" cure
• Conducted immediately after the social error	
• Conducted by any significant adult	
• Generally held in a one-on-one session	

Situation, Options, Consequences, Choices, Strategies, Simulation

The Situation, Options, Consequences, Choices, Strategies, Simulation (SOCCSS) strategy was developed to help students with social interaction problems put social and behavioral issues into a sequential form (Roosa, personal communication). The strategy helps students understand problem situations and lets them see that they have to make choices about a given situation and that each choice has a given consequence. The SOCCSS strategy works as follows:

SITUATION: When a social problem arises, the teacher works with the student to identify the situation. Together they define the problem and state a goal. The stage occurs through discussion, writing, and drawings.

OPTIONS: Following identification of the situation, the student and teacher brainstorm several options for behavior. At this point, the teacher accepts all student responses and does not evaluate them. Typically, the options are listed in written or pictorial format. According to Spivak, Platt, and Shure (1976), this step is critical to problem-solving. The ability to generate multiple solutions diminishes student frustration, encourages them to see more than one perspective, and results in student resiliency.

CONSEQUENCES: The student and teacher work together to evaluate each of the options generated. Kaplan and Carter (1995) suggest that each of the options be evaluated using the following two criteria: (a) Efficacy–Will the solution get me what I want? and (b) Feasibility–Will I be able to do it? Each of the consequences is labeled with an **E** for efficacy or **F** for feasibility. The teacher works as a facilitator, using pointed questions to help the student develop consequences for each option without dictating consequences.

CHOICES: The student then prioritizes the options and consequences and selects a solution from the list of generated options. The student-selected option is the one that has the most desirable consequences.

STRATEGIES: The student and adult work together to develop a plan of action. Although the adult may provide guidance by asking leading questions or making suggestions, the student should ultimately develop the plan so that he has ownership.

SIMULATION: The student is given an opportunity to turn the abstract strategy into something more concrete either through role-play, imagery, talking with a peer about the plan, or writing or typing the plan.

Figure 3.3 provides a worksheet that can be used to facilitate the SOCCSS process.

SOCCSS

Situation, Options, Consequences, Choices, Strategies, Simulation

Situation

Who _____

What _____

_____

_____

When _____

Why _____

Options

Consequences

Choice

Strategy – Plan of Action

Figure 3.3. SOCCSS.

Simulation	Select One
1. Find a quiet place, sit back and imagine how your *Situation* would work (or not work) based on the various *Options and Consequences*.	
2. Talk with a peer, staff, or other person about your plan of action.	
3. Write down on paper what may happen in your *Situation* based on your *Options and Consequences*.	
4. Practice your *Options* with one or more people using behavior rehearsal.	
5. _____	

Simulation Outcomes

Follow-Up

Figure 3.3. Continued

Created by Myles, 1998, from the work of Roosa, J. B. (1995). *Men on the move: Competence and cooperation "Conflict resolution and beyond."* Kansas City, MO: Author.

Video Detective

Videos or television, if monitored for content, can serve as excellent instructional tools. One mother teaches her son about nonverbal communication by using *Saved by the Bell*, a television program about high school students. After she has introduced a concept, she plays the taped television show with the sound turned down and asks the student to predict the actors' nonverbal and verbal communication messages based on what he sees on the screen. Similarly, a middle school teacher routinely videotapes her class during planned simulations and regular activities and uses the tapes as instructional tools. Students can see themselves giving mixed messages using ineffective verbal strategies to communicate to others, and can monitor their voice tone or proximity. The teacher works with small groups of students to create scripts that the students act out on video. She plays the videotaped scripts and hosts two game show-type activities for her student contestants, "What's My Emotion" and "Find the Conversation Flaw."

Care should be taken when selecting videos or television shows that children with Asperger Syndrome may use as models. Because of their highly visual format, these shows may teach skills that were not intended. One young man learned social skills from *Walker, Texas Ranger*, a show that features a law enforcement officer who often battles his opponents using karate. Our young friend's interpretation of the show: "If you don't get what you like or if someone is doing something bad, kick them. Then you will be a hero."

Restructuring

Restructuring or modifying the environment is a lifelong requirement for most persons with Asperger Syndrome. Varying degrees of restructuring are required based on student skill levels and learning styles. In most cases, as persons with Asperger Syndrome become older, they are able to provide the modifications for themselves or they can request that they be implemented. Restructuring includes the use of social scripts, visual supports, circle of friends and crafting the environment.

Social Scripts

Children and youth with Asperger Syndrome may benefit from having adults structure their responses through the use of scripts. Social scripts provide ready-to-use language for specific events. They may be structured as conversation starters, scripted responses, or cues to change topic. For instance, a child may practice a script that includes key questions that can help him begin a conversation with another child. For the child who has trouble spontaneously generating language, social scripts are an effective intervention because they help with language recall and assist the child in taking on another's perspective. This option minimizes stress associated with approaching peers because it reduces the probability of an unpredictable event occurring. Table 3.7 provides an example of a social script for a young man with Asperger Syndrome

Table 3.7
Sample Social Script

Scenario

Jeremy frequently experienced difficulty when attempting to join his fourth-grade peers at recess. Without an invitation, Jeremy would barge into the group game and demand to be the center of attention and take the role of what he considered to be the key player. That is, he wanted to be the pitcher in baseball, the quarterback in football or the goalie in soccer. When peers told Jeremy to wait his turn or not to play with them, Jeremy would wrestle the ball away from a peer and make his peers chase him. On several occasions, fights resulted from this type of interaction.

A social script was developed to assist Jeremy in acting appropriately when joining and participating in group games. Jeremy was coached in the use of the script, and in the early stages of its use he was accompanied by his teacher. Over time, the teacher faded his presence and Jeremy used the script independently.

Social Script

When I want to join a game at recess, I will stand near the children playing the game, but not on the field or in the way of the players. I will say, "Can I join in your game?" If my friends say that I can, I will ask, "What position is open?" When I am in the game, I will follow the rules. If my friends tell me not to play because the game has already started or for some other reason, I will say, "OK, but I would like to play next time."

Visual Supports

As mentioned, students with Asperger Syndrome benefit from information presented visually rather than auditorally. Visual information is more concrete than auditory information and allows for greater processing time.

Visual schedules

Visual schedules take an abstract concept such as time and present it in a more concrete and manageable form. As such, they can yield multiple benefits for children and youth with Asperger Syndrome who often exhibit visual strengths. For example, visual schedules allow students to anticipate upcoming events and activities, develop an understanding of time and facilitate the ability to predict change. Further, they can be utilized to stimulate communicative exchanges through a discussion of past, present, and future events; increase on-task behavior; facilitate transition between activities; and teach new skills.

Students may enjoy and feel more comfortable when allowed to participate in preparing their own schedule. This should occur first thing in the morning. Students can assist in assembling their schedule, copying it, or adding their own personal touch in some other manner. This interactive time can also be used to review the daily routine, discuss changes, and reinforce rules.

Figure 3.4 provides samples of two visual schedules for students with Asperger Syndrome. If the student is concerned about looking or acting differently from others in the classroom, care should be taken to ensure that the visual schedule fits easily into the child's environment without attracting too much attention. Credit card-sized or bookmark-formatted visual schedules provide structure, but can be used discreetly.

Graphic organizers

Graphic organizers, such as semantic maps, Venn diagrams, outlines, and compare/contrast charts, provide visual, holistic representations of facts and concepts and their relationship within an organized framework. That is, these strategies arrange key terms to show their relationship to each other, presenting abstract or implicit information in a concrete manner. They are particularly useful with content area material such as social studies, science, and so on. Graphic organizers can be used before, during or after students read a selection, either as an advance organizer or as a measure of concept attainment following reading.

Graphic organizers often enhance the learning of students with Asperger Syndrome because:

1. They are visual, and this modality is often a strength for students.
2. They are static; they remain consistent and constant.
3. They allow for processing time; the student can reflect on the material at his own pace.
4. They are concrete and are more easily understood than a verbal-only presentation.

Figure 3.5 provides some examples of graphic organizers that may be effective for children and youth with Asperger Syndrome.

Timelines

Timelines are another important form of visual support for children and youth with Asperger Syndrome. Timelines break down assignments into their component parts and set deadlines for their completion. Because children and youth with Asperger Syndrome often have difficulty with the concept of time, many think they can read a novel and write a 10-page paper the night before it is due. Other individuals with Asperger Syndrome simply cannot get started when they are given a complex task; they do not know, without assistance, how to break it down into smaller pieces. As a result, they spend the entire time worrying about getting the assignment done and do not have a strategy to begin and/or complete the task.

Maps

Maps are extremely important for persons with Asperger Syndrome, particularly at the middle school and high school levels. Often these individuals cannot visualize where their locker is in reference to classes. For example, Josefa, a middle school student with Asperger Syndrome, was on the verge of serving detention time for being consistently late to classes. I followed Josefa throughout her school day to determine the reason for her tardiness. Very simply, Josefa was late to class because she went to her locker during each 10-minute passing time. This caused problems. For example, second- and third-period classes were in the west wing of the building, her locker was in the east wing. Instead of going to her locker after the first period and gathering her books for the subsequent two periods, Josefa would race from the west wing to the east wing, then back to the west wing. I gave her a map of the school showing her the most efficient ways to get from class to class and

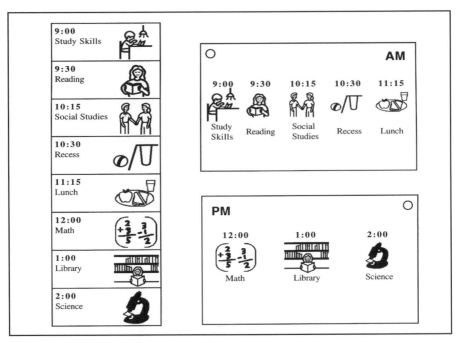

Figure 3.4. Sample visual schedules.

Schedules made with the Boardmaker™ and the Picture Communication Symbols. The Picture Communication Symbols © 1981-1999 are used with permission from the Mayer-Johnson Company, P.O. Box 1579, Solana Beach, CA 92075, 619-550-0084 (phone), 619-550-0449 (fax), and Mayerj@mayer-johnson.com (email).

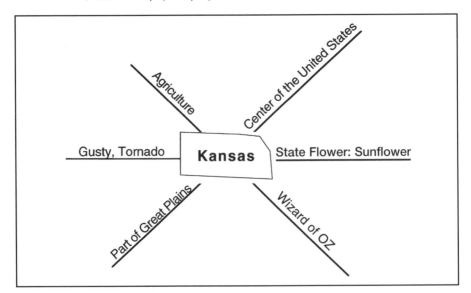

Figure 3.5. Sample graphic organizers.

what books she should take with her each time she went to her locker. She told me that, first of all, she had no idea that there was more than one way to get to any class and, second, she did not realize that it made more sense for her not to visit her locker between every class.

Circle of Friends

Helping students develop friendships and support networks is often integral to their school success. Because the desire for social interactions is typically high, involving the student with Asperger Syndrome with peers usually serves as a strong motivator. In addition, it provides an excellent venue for students to practice social skills that they may have learned from adults in direct instruction situations. Students should be paired with socially astute and compliant buddies. Individuals who enjoy the way the person with Asperger Syndrome looks at life are excellent candidates for a circle of friends. Those who participate in the circle must value the person with Asperger Syndrome, not merely placate her and dictate her activities. Establishing a "lunch bunch" is one way of using a circle of friends. In a lunch bunch three to four students eat together. The child with Asperger Syndrome, as a part of the lunch bunch, might bring with her a card of conversation starters or questions that she can ask. The peers interact with her as a friend, helping her participate in lunch conversation. After eating, the lunch bunch might engage in a structured activity, such as a game.

Crafting the Environment

Environmental supports can enhance student functioning in the social and academic sense. Children and youth with Asperger Syndrome, as well as all children, need an appropriate curriculum tailored to their often uneven skill profiles. They require structured activities that allow them to show their skills. Students who appear to have learning disabilities or similar characteristics may be given strategy instruction to facilitate skill acquisition. For example, because of slow processing time, they may complete only the even-numbered items on a math worksheet. Because of motor difficulties, they are permitted to take a test verbally or to type a book report on the computer. When notetaking is required, a peer takes notes using carbon paper and gives the duplicate to the student with Asperger Syndrome. The student who experiences problems with unaided recall may take a multiple-choice test instead of a short-answer or essay examination. The person who has trouble functioning successfully in cooperative groups is given a specific role in the group (i.e., timekeeper) or initially participates in peer tutoring sessions. Or the individual with Asperger Syndrome whose organizational skills make it difficult for homework to get home has a homework hotline buddy who helps her remember what assignments are due.

Adults working with these children should continually ask, "What can be done to make the environment more understandable for my student? How can I help her be more successful?" It is the ultimate goal to help individuals with Asperger Syndrome understand their exceptionality, complete with its strengths and challenges. From this understanding will come an awareness of the modifications the individual needs in order to be successful. The student with Asperger Syndrome can then be taught to be active in putting into place modifications that will help her demonstrate her skills in a positive way.

Summary

Helping students with Asperger Syndrome increase and enhance skills relative to self-awareness, self-calming, and self-management requires a multifaceted approach. These individuals require instruction on social, behavioral, and academic skills; interpretation of their environment; and restructuring to ensure that their individual needs are met. With appropriate support through these means, individuals with Asperger Syndrome will not need to resort to rage as their only option for communicating their wants and needs.

CHAPTER 4

Specifically for Parents

C hildren and youth with Asperger Syndrome offer their parents many joys and many challenges. How parents view challenges related to behavior and home routines often impacts how the child reacts to these situations. Parents need to work together to develop a home plan that addresses the following issues: (a) agreement on the causes of problem behaviors, (b) family organization and support, (c) the LASTING word, and (d) designing a daily routine. Each of these areas can be challenging, but when a working system is created, both the child and parents are more satisfied.

Agreement on the Causes of Problem Behaviors

Frequently, parents and other caregivers disagree on how much, if any, of the behavior exhibited by the child with Asperger Syndrome is voluntary. One parent may firmly believe that the behavior is under the child's control and, thus, require discipline to effect a change. The other parent, on the other hand, may see the behavior as part of the syndrome and firmly state that discipline should not be used.

Even though the parents may not hold identical views on the behavior, they are often unaware of the differences in their views. In fact, one or both of the parents may become stronger in their beliefs to compensate for the other's behaviors. The result is arguments between the parents regarding how to parent the child. Often the child senses this difference and uses it to pit one parent against the other, resulting in increased behavior problems exhibited by the child.

Unless the adults reach a joint understanding and acceptance of the cause of a given behavior, the child will not learn new skills and the caregivers will only become further polarized in their attempts to parent the child.

It is likely that many of the behaviors manifested by the child are neurological in nature and are a part of the exceptionality known as Asperger Syndrome. But how can parents confirm this? First, read several books on Asperger Syndrome; attempt to identify similarities in behavior patterns delineated in those books and those of your child. Second, attend parent support group meetings. Listen to other parents. Are they experiencing similar problems? Third, talk to the child's teachers. Under similar circumstances and in similar environments, does the child engage in the behavior? If you find the same types of behaviors described in any of these three settings, at least some of the behaviors exhibited by your child are most likely neurologically based. Caregivers within the family should discuss and then agree on which behaviors are chosen and which are a part of Asperger Syndrome. Then they can agree on which behaviors they will attempt to modify and which types of interventions they will use.

Family Organization and Support

Asperger Syndrome affects the entire family. Raising a child with this exceptionality is labor intensive. It takes more time, attention, energy, and skill to raise such a child. At times, it is frustrating and exhausting. It takes a family to parent a child with Asperger Syndrome. In two-parent families, both individuals need to devote themselves to supporting each other, their child with Asperger Syndrome, and other children. In single-parent families, extended families and friends take on an important role, providing support and assistance as needed.

Many parents find it helpful to join a support group. Some of these groups provide childcare while the parents meet. In addition to gaining support from other parents, there are opportunities to learn new strategies that will help the entire family. Some support group families become extended families, providing advice and listening at critical times.

Parents also need to consider respite. That is, they need time away from their child. All parents need time to have an identity outside of being a parent. They need time to go to a movie, go to the library, or just relax without their primary concern being the child. For parents, respite offers the opportunity to relax and re-energize, which is in the best interest of the whole family. For the child with Asperger Syndrome, respite offers an opportunity to have new experiences and generalize skills across people and environments. In a respite care situation, with a trained babysitter or care provider, the child can practice skills and learn flexibility by beginning to recognize that different people have different expectations.

The LASTING Word

Altercations between parents and children are a given. People who live in a family that has a member with Asperger Syndrome often have more occasions for problem behavior in the rumbling stage as well as the rage stage. Often the rage cycle is exacerbated by the "last word." It seems that many children with Asperger Syndrome need to have the "last word" in any discussion or exchange; many parents, however, believe that the last word should always rest with them. Thus, arguments go on interminably and often escalate to outbursts of rage.

To stop this cycle, consider the concept of the "LASTING Word." In setting up this strategy, parents need to provide direction. One rule of thumb is to:

1. Say what you mean—mean what you say.
2. Say it only twice in a calm voice.
3. Verify the child's understanding. If the child processes information visually, the parent may need to choose her words carefully. Consider using icons or pictures to facilitate understanding.
4. Stop talking and take action.

Remember, it is not important to have the last word, but it is imperative that parents have the LASTING word. In this way, children will learn to understand that they can count on parents to help set boundaries for them and enforce limitations.

Designing a Daily Routine

As many children with Asperger Syndrome do not have that inner clock that provides self-organization, it is important that parents create a daily plan. This plan will aid the entire family in getting along and meeting the many and diverse requirements of their day. The plan is fluid. Although it is built around a basic structure, it will require modifications as schedules change and as the child develops new skills. It is critical that the plan is a family plan. Family members should work together to create the plan as well as decide when it should be reviewed and modified. Parents should also understand that there will be times when they will "blow it." That is when, for some reason, they will not follow the plan. Part of the family plan should include how to handle these exceptions and how to get back into the routine once it has been broken.

Morning Routine

It is common for children to have difficulty getting up in the morning. Often this problem is more marked for children and youth with Asperger Syndrome, who seem to experience particular difficulty in adjusting to change (i.e., from sleep to awake; from recess to silent reading time). Young children who are awakened by their parents may require several wake-up calls and seem to do better with this type of gradual transition between sleep and awake.

As the child becomes older, she assumes more responsibility for getting up. Some families have found the two-alarm clock method to be helpful. A snooze alarm with music, set 30 minutes before actual get-up time, is placed near the child's bed. When it sounds, the child may turn off the snooze alarm and keep sleeping for the 10-minute intervals between the musical interludes. A second alarm, which provides a loud and clamorous sound, sits across the room from the child's bed. It is set to go off at the actual get-up time. When this second alarm sounds, the child must go across the room to turn it off. An important part of the success of this structure is to teach the child to shower immediately after turning off the second alarm.

Even when the child is awake, she may not be in a complete state of alertness or arousal. Underarousal results in the child moping around. She exhibits low effort and motivation, lacks attention, has difficulty focusing and problems processing information. Parents dealing with this type of child should use a calm voice, keep directs simple, and instruct in doing one thing at a time. Overarousal, on the other hand, results in the child being irritable and quick to anger. She often has difficulty remembering things and does not think clearly. Parents of an overaroused child should say as little as possible and refrain from assigning tasks that require clear thinking. They might want to consider the use of a home base (see Chapter 2) to help calm the child, as needed.

Dressing is another frequent problem in the morning routine. Alertness problems may cause inattention in selecting clothes. As a result, how the clothes look or feel sometimes becomes an issue. It is often a good idea to have the child select clothes the night before to minimize any problems related to arousal level.

Many children with Asperger Syndrome experience organizational difficulties and, consequently, have a difficult time collecting all materials needed for school in the morning. Habitual learning of the care of homework, the back pack, lunch box, and other school materials is necessary. Many parents have posted near the door a visual schedule that shows all items needed for school. Children, as a part of their bed time ritual, locate and pack all school materials.

Questions related to developing a morning strategy include:

1. How can a smooth transition between sleep and awake be structured?
2. How will the parent know if the child is under- or overaroused?
3. How will the parent react to the child when he is in each of these stages?
4. What steps are needed to help the child complete the morning routine?
5. Do visual supports or preparing the night before help the child complete the morning routine successfully?

The Rage Cycle

Although the rage cycle was discussed at length in Chapter 2, there are some specific considerations for parents whose children have rage attacks, meltdowns, and neurological storms. Each child's rage cycle has a pattern–the rumbling stage occurs first, followed by the rage attack, meltdown, or neurological storm. Some of the prominent characteristics at each stage are:

1. During the rumbling stage, the child exhibits a pattern of behaviors that build. These behaviors may include biting nails or lips, lowering the voice, tensing muscles, tapping the foot, grimacing, or other indications of general discontent.
2. There is typically a sudden onset of the rage.
3. Quite often the behavior appears to be unprovoked; however, there *is* a cause.
4. The rage is grossly out of proportion to the situation.
5. The child gets no pleasure from the behavior, is often remorseful afterwards, and wants the episodes to stop.

6. During the rage cycle, the child is not thinking rationally. Thus, reasoning with the child at this stage does not work.

Often the best thing to do is to attempt to implement some of the techniques described in Chapter 2 if the behavior is in the rumbling stage (e.g., antiseptic bouncing; "just walk and don't talk"). If the child is in the rumbling stage or early stages of the rage attack, assisting the child to a safe room is one of the best options. In the safe room, the child can relax so that she can once again have control. The safe room is not a disciplinary procedure; it is an area in the home that contains stress-reducing activities that help the child refocus.

Parents need to plan a strategy for a graceful exit for the child when they see escalation building. The child may not have sufficient emotional maturity to read his own internal clues and will rely on the parent to cue that the rage cycle has begun. By carefully observing the child, the pattern of signals exhibited during the rumbling stage can be identified. If, by agreement, the parent and child have developed a nonintrusive sign that the safe room is needed, the child can be signaled.

Sometimes during a rage attack, the child will cling to the parent. It is important that parents disengage from the child in a calm and unemotional manner. The parent may need to make comments such as, "I know this is hard for you," "No matter what, I love you," or "It is time to work through this." Remember, the least said, the better. The child is not thinking rationally and parents' immediate goal should be to get out of the storm.

The following questions should be asked relative to the rage cycle:

1. What behaviors does the child exhibit during the rumbling stage?
2. What strategies will the parent use during this stage?
3. What behaviors does the child exhibit during the rage stage?
4. What strategies will the parent use during this stage?
5. Where will the safe room be located in the home?
6. How will the child be directed there?
7. What strategies can the parent use to disengage from the child who is in the rage cycle?

Chores

It is important that all family members have home-based responsibilities. Some children resist chores so much that it becomes easier for the parent to do them, but this is often not in the best developmental interest of the child.

As a first step, parents should select one chore for their child to complete; initially, they may have to work along with the child to complete it. Pick a task that the child would like the most or, at least, resist the least. Even when the child can do more than one chore, the list should remain simple. Trying to remember several things at the same time is difficult. A task list posted on the refrigerator often is a good strategy to help students fulfill their chore responsibilities.

Parents cannot assume that the child knows how to do even the most simple chore. Consequently, the parent must model the chore, work alongside the child several times until independence is achieved, or make a visual display of the steps needed to complete the chore. If the chore is not completed to parent satisfaction, fault finding is not a good way to improve performance. Neither is the temptation for the parent to redo the task. Instead, it is best for the parent and child to work through the chore together.

It is typically helpful to the child if a time frame for chore completion is established. Such a time frame should allow the child some flexibility, with completion tied to some natural event. For example, the child needs to complete the chore before watching television. This type of structure also serves as a natural consequence if the task is not completed.

Parents should ask themselves the following questions when assigning and monitoring chores:

1. What chores are reasonable for the child to complete?
2. What is the best way to teach the child to do the tasks?
3. What will time completion expectations look like?
4. What will happen if the chores are not completed properly?

After-School Hours

For children with Asperger Syndrome, the hours immediately following school are often the most difficult because the children are likely to be stress-filled and fatigued. These emotional states may be the result of trying hard to "hold it together during school hours" or of a difficult, disappointing day. The children may also be overstimulated from the school environment. The result is that the child with Asperger Syndrome often engages in tantrumming, crying, or withdrawal. These are the "arsenic hours."

Experience and careful observation typically indicate the best way to handle the "arsenic hours." Some children do better when they engage in a physical activity immediately after school. Parents consequently schedule dance, karate, swimming or other activities to occur immediately upon leaving school. Other children do better if they have quiet time alone; this may include working on a computer, drawing, or taking a nap. To complicate matters, some children feel the need to change their after-school activities every few days, because their preferences or desired interests frequently change.

Some issues to be addressed relative to after-school hours include:

1. What activities work best immediately after school?
2. How can parents encourage the child to engage in these activities?

Homework

Distractibility, lack of organizational skills, and difficulty with handwriting are only three of the difficulties many children and youth with Asperger Syndrome experience to make homework completion problematic. Any or all of these characteristics combine to lengthen the time required to complete homework. When an extended length of time is required, fatigue and the desire to watch television, for example, add to the potential for behavior problems.

Most schools recommend a certain amount of homework each evening. Parents and teachers should work together to ensure that the requirements for homework are not too intensive for the child. Children with Asperger Syndrome should not be required to spend the majority of their evening hours doing homework.

Distractibility can often be reduced by having an established routine that includes the same study hour and the same study place each day with all materials available. It is often best if the child is not in the vicinity of other playing children or the television. The attention span of the child will dictate whether one long or several short segments should be structured for homework completion. Sometimes, the child's attention span can be expanded if an adult is present in the same room reading or engaging in an otherwise nonintrusive activity.

Because of their child's *inherent lack of organizational skills*, parents often have to help their children get started on homework by providing a structure for work completion. Depending on the needs of the child, parent structure can be as simple as asking, "What must you do first?" or as complex as creating a list of steps of what must be done.

The issue of motor skills should also be a consideration for the child with Asperger Syndrome. The child who has *poor handwriting* or who cannot complete a page without numerous erasures may need some accommodations. The use of a computer or dictating to a parent or into a tape recorder may be options that help in homework completion.

The following issues should be addressed regarding homework completion:

1. What blocks the child from completing homework successfully?
2. What does the homework routine look like?
3. What interferes with homework completion? How can these interferences be minimized?
4. Should breaks be incorporated into the homework period? If so, how often should they occur, how long should they last, and what activities should be available to the child?
5. If organization is a problem, how can the parent help structure the child?
6. What accommodations should be made for homework completion?
7. Which caregiver can best help with which homework subjects?

Bedtime

Many children with Asperger Syndrome suffer from sleep disturbances. These may be manifested as (a) difficulties going to bed, (b) problems staying asleep or sleep walking, and (c) requiring more or less sleep than others.

One of the first questions to be resolved is whether bedtime should be set by a clock or the fatigue level of the child. Most parents have some concept of a graduating bedtime based on the age of the child, but this does not always work with children and youth with Asperger Syndrome.

Some parents allow their children to set their own bedtimes when they are tired enough to give in to sleep. Other parents select a bedtime for their child. If the child is not ready to sleep at the predetermined time, she is allowed to complete quiet activities in bed (i.e., coloring, reading, listening to calming music). Whatever strategy is selected, enough sleep time needs to be structured so that the child can get up in the morning and get prepared for the day with few problems.

Transitioning to bedtime is often a problem for children and youth with Asperger Syndrome. Many require an advance warning. Sometimes a quiet activity such as playing a quiet game with a parent or reading a book are good options to precede bedtime. Some parents and children use this transition as a quiet one-on-one time to simply enjoy each other's company.

If the child resists sleep, it is important to investigate the underlying causes. These may include, but are not limited to: (a) bedtime fears, (b) obsessive thoughts that will not stop, (c) bedtime compulsions, (d) wanting to be with parents, (e) wanting to have the same bedtime as older siblings, or (f) reaction to medication. Each situation is dealt with differently. For example, if bedtime compulsions are a problem, then reading or listening to music may help them subside. If medication is a problem, a consultation with the child's physician may lead to changing the dosage or the time the child takes the medication.

The following should be considered relative to bedtime:

1. What should set bedtime: child fatigue or a predetermined time?
2. How can the child be transitioned into bedtime?
3. What is the bedtime routine?
4. If the child resists bedtime, what is the cause? What can be done to minimize this resistance?

Summary

There are many issues that must be addressed head-on to help children and youth function at home and enjoy their parents and siblings. Parents must provide a structure compatible with their own needs and the needs of other family members to help the person with Asperger Syndrome function appropriately and happily within the family. Although it takes a lot of work to develop this type of plan, the rewards are numerous for the entire family.

References

Adams, J. I. (1997). *Autism-P.D.D.: More creative ideas from age eight to early adulthood.* Ontario: Adams Publications.

Albert, L. (1989). *A teacher's guide to cooperative discipline: How to manage your classroom and promote self-esteem.* Circle Pines, MN: American Guidance Service.

American Psychological Association. (1994). *Diagnostic and statistical manual of mental disorders* (4th ed.). Washington, DC: Author.

Anderson, E., & Emmons, P. (1996). *Unlocking the mysteries of sensory dysfunction: A resource for anyone who works with or lives with a child with sensory issues.* Austin, TX: Future Horizons.

Arwood, E. L. (1991). *Semantic and pragmatic language disorders* (2nd ed.). Denver, CO: Aspen.

Asperger, H. (1944). Die 'Autistichen Psychopathen' im Kindersalter. *Archiv für Psychiatrie und Nervenkrankheiten, 117,* 76-136.

Attwood, T. (1998). *Asperger's Syndrome: A guide for parents and professionals.* London: Jessica Kinglsey.

Autism Asperger Resource Center. (1997). *Assessing the setting demands in the classroom.* Kansas City, KS: Author.

Ayres, J. (1979). *Sensory integration and the child.* Los Angeles: Western Psychological Services.

Baron-Cohen, S. (1988). An assessment of violence in a young man with Asperger's Syndrome. *Journal of Child Psychology and Psychiatry, 29*(3), 351-360.

Baron-Cohen, S., Allen, J., & Gillberg, C. (1992). Can autism be detected at 18 months? The needle, the haystack, and the CHAT. *British Journal of Psychiatry, 161,* 839-843.

Baron-Cohen, S., Jolliffe, T., Mortimore, C., & Robertson, M. (1997). Another advanced test of theory of mind: Evidence from very high functioning adults with autism or Asperger Syndrome. *Journal of Child Psychology and Psychiatry, 38*(7), 813-822.

Beck, M. (1985). Understanding and managing the acting-out child. *The Pointer, 29*(2), 27-29.

Berthier, M., Santamaria, J., Encabo, H., & Tolosa, E. (1992). Recurrent hypersomnia in two adolescent males with Asperger's Syndrome. *Journal of the American Academy of Child and Adolescent Psychiatry, 31*(4), 735-738.

Bieber, J. (Producer). (1994). *Learning disabilities and social skills with Richard LaVoie: Last one picked ... first one picked on.* Washington, DC: Public Broadcasting Service.

Cumine, V., Leach, J., & Stevenson, F. (1998). *Asperger Syndrome: A practical guide for teachers.* London: David Fulton.

Duke, M. P., Nowicki, S., & Martin, E. A. (1996). *Teaching your child the language of social success.* Atlanta, GA: Peachtree.

Durand, V. M., & Crimmins, D. (1992). *Motivation assessment scale.* Topeka, KS: Monaco & Associates.

Ehlers, S., & Gillberg, C. (1993). The epidemiology of Asperger Syndrome. A total population study. *Journal of Child Psychology and Psychiatry, 34*(8), 1327-1350.

Frith, U. (1991). *Autism and Asperger Syndrome.* Cambridge: Cambridge University Press.

Gath, A. (1989). Theory and therapy of psychosis in childhood: Experience in England. *Italian Journal of Intellective Impairment, 2*(2), 123-130.

Ghaziuddin, N., Metler, L., Ghaziuddin, M., Tsai, L., & Giordani, B. (1993). Three siblings with Asperger Syndrome: A family case study. *European Child and Adolescent Psychiatry, 2*(1), 44-49.

Gillberg, C. (1993). Autism and related behaviors. *Journal of Intellectual Disability Research, 37,* 343-372.

Gillberg, I. C., & Gillberg, C. (1989). Asperger Syndrome–Some epidemiological considerations: A research note. *Journal of Child Psychology and Psychiatry, 30*(4), 631-638.

Grandin, T. (1999, April). *Understanding people with autism: Developing a career makes life satisfying.* Paper presented at the MAAP Services, Incorporated, and Indiana Resource Center for Autism Conference, Indianapolis, IN.

Gray, C. (1994, October). *Making sense out of the world: Social stories, comic strip conversations, and related instructional techniques.* Paper presented at the Midwest Educational Leadership Conference on Autism, Kansas City, MO.

Gray, C. (1995). *Social stories unlimited: Social stories and comic strip conversations.* Jenison, MI: Jenison Public Schools.

Gray, C., & Gerand, J. D. (1993). Social stories: Improving responses of students with autism with accurate social information. *Focus on Autistic Behavior, 8,* 1-10.

Hadwin, J., Baron-Cohen, S., Howlin, P., & Hill, K. (1996). Can we teach children with autism to understand emotions, belief, or pretence? *Development and Psychopathology, 8,* 345-365.

Howlin, P., Baron-Cohen, S., & Hadwin, J. (1999). *Teaching children with autism to mind-read: A practical guide.* New York: John Wiley & Sons.

Jordan, R., & Powell, S. (1995). *Understanding and teaching children with autism.* New York: John Wiley.

Kaplan, J. S., & Carter, J. (1995). *Beyond behavior modification: A cognitive-behavioral approach to management in the school* (3rd ed.) Austin, TX: Pro-Ed.

Kern, L., Dunlap, G., Clarke, S., & Childs, K. (1994). Student-assisted functional assessment interview. *Diagnostique, 19*(2-3), 29-39.

Kerr, M. M., & Nelson, C. M. (1993). *Strategies for managing behavior problems in the classroom.* Columbus, OH: Merrill/Macmillan.

Klin, A. (1999, March). *Asperger's Syndrome: An update on clinical research: Clinical features and neuropsychology.* Conference on Asperger's Syndrome and Related Conditions, New Haven, CT.

Kozleski, E. B. (1991). Visual symbol acquisition by students with autism. *Exceptionality, 2,* 173-194.

Krantz, P. J., MacDuff, M. T., & McClannahan, L. E. (1993). Programming participation in family activities for children with autism: Parents' use of photographic activity schedules. *Journal of Applied Behavior Analysis, 26,* 89-97.

Kuttler, S., Myles, B. S., & Carlson, J. K. (1998). The use of social stories to reduce precursors to tantrum behavior in a student with autism. *Focus on Autism and Other Developmental Disabilities, 13*(3), 176-182.

Leslie, A. M. (1987). Pretense and representation: The origins of a "theory of mind." *Psychological Review, 97,* 122-131.

Leslie, A. M., & Frith, U. (1988). Autistic children's understanding of seeing, knowing, and believing. *British Journal of Developmental Psychology, 6,* 315-324.

Lewis, T. J., Scott, T. M., & Sugai, G. (1994). The problem behavior questionnaire: A teacher-based instrument to develop functional hypotheses of problem behavior in general education classrooms. *Diagnostique, 19*(2-3), 103-115.

Long, N. J., Morse, W. C., & Newman, R. G. (1976). *Conflict in the classroom: The educational children with problems* (3rd ed.). Belmont, CA: Wadsworth.

McConnell, M. E., Hilvitz, P. B., & Cox, C. J. (1998). Functional assessment: A systematic process for assessment and intervention in general and special education classrooms. *Intervention in School and Clinic, 34*(1), 10-20.

Meara, K., Brandt, J., & Myles, B. S. (in press). Central auditory processing in five persons with Asperger Syndrome. *Focus on Autism and Other Developmental Disabilities.*

Myles, B. S., & Simpson, R. L. (1998). *Asperger Syndrome: A guide for educators and parents.* Austin, TX: Pro-Ed.

Myles, B. S., Simpson, R. L., & Becker, J. (1994-1995). An analysis of characteristics of students diagnosed with higher-functioning autistic disorder. *Exceptionality, 5*(1), 19-30.

Myles, B. S., Simpson, R. L., & Bock, S. J. (1999). *Asperger Syndrome diagnostic test.* Manuscript in preparation.

O'Neill, R. E., Horner, R. H., Albin, R. W., Sprague, J. R., Storey, K., & Newton, J. S. (1997). *Functional assessment and program development for problem behavior: A practical handbook* (2nd ed.). Albany, NY: Brooks/Cole.

Orr, S., Myles, B. S., & Dunn, W. (1999). *Sensory profiles of children and youth with Asperger Syndrome.* Manuscript in preparation.

Quill, K. A. (1995). *Teaching children with autism: Strategies to enhance communication and socialization.* New York: Delmar Publishers.

Rogers, M. F., & Myles, B. S. (1999). *Using social stories and comic strip conversations to interpret social situations for a young man with Asperger Syndrome.* Manuscript in preparation.

Simblett, G. J., & Wilson, D. N. (1993). Asperger's Syndrome: Three cases and a discussion. *Journal of Intellectual Disability Research, 37,* 85-97

Spivack, G., Platt, J. J., & Shure, M. (1976). *The problem-solving approach to adjustment.* San Francisco: Jossey-Bass.

Swaggart, B., Gagnon, E., Bock, S., Earles, T., Quinn, C., Myles, B. S., & Simpson, R. (1995). Using social stories to teach social and behavioral skills to children with autism. *Focus on Autistic Behavior, 10,* 1-16.

Szatmari, P., Bremner, R., & Nagy, J. (1989). Asperger's Syndrome: A review of clinical features. *Canadian Journal of Psychiatry, 34*(6), 554-560.

Valentine, M. R. (1987). *How to deal with discipline problems in the schools: A practical guide for educators.* Dubuque, IA: Kendall Hunt.

Williams, K. (1995). Understanding the student with Asperger Syndrome: Guidelines for teachers. *Focus on Autistic Behavior, 10*(2), 9-16.

Williams, M.S., & Shellenberger, S. (1996). *How does your engine run: A leader's guide to the alert program for self-regulation.* Albuquerque, NM: TherapyWorks, Inc.

Wing, L. (1981). Asperger's Syndrome: A clinical account. *Psychological Medicine, 11,* 115-129.

World Health Organization. (1992). *International classification of diseases and related health problems* (10th ed.). Geneva, Switzerland: Author.

Index